Moving into the Express Lane

Moving into the Express Lane

How to Rapidly Increase the Value of Your Business

Rick Pay

BEP BUSINESS EXPERT PRESS

Moving into the Express Lane: How to Rapidly Increase the Value of Your Business

First published in 2018 by
Business Expert Press, LLC
222 East 46th Street, New York, NY 10017
www.businessexpertpress.com

ISBN-13: 978-1-63157-843-4 (paperback)
ISBN-13: 978-1-63157-844-1 (e-book)

Business Expert Press Supply and Operations Management Collection

Collection ISSN: 2156-8189 (print)
Collection ISSN: 2156-8200 (electronic)

Cover and interior design by Exeter Premedia Services Private Ltd., Chennai, India

First edition: 2018

10 9 8 7 6 5 4 3 2 1

Printed in the United States of America.

This book is dedicated to my Growth Cycle, a group of high-powered consultants who have helped me move into the express lanes of my business—Alan Weiss, Val Wright, Lorraine Moore, Lisa McLeod, Amanda Setili, and Connie Dieken. Your inspiration has moved me to new heights. And of course Paige McKinney, without whom this book would not exist.

Abstract

Moving into the Express Lane: How to Rapidly Increase the Value of Your Business will show readers how to rapidly and exponentially increase their company's value by aligning operations strategy with the business model. Increasing a business's value and potential sale price is important for business transitions as well as for ongoing business operations to accelerate revenue growth, increase profits and cash flow, and to allow the company to increase capacity and grow without capital expense. Many companies focus too much on implementing tactics such as Lean without a strategic framework, which renders their efforts fruitless. By instead taking a holistic operations-based view of strategy and tactics, executives can exponentially improve their company's value. This book is based on the analogy of the express or high-occupancy vehicle lanes on a freeway, where vehicles move much faster than the other lanes where traffic is moving slowly or not at all.

The concepts and concrete resources in *Moving into the Express Lane* are useful to manufacturing, distribution, and retail organizations, as well as any company that has an operations component and suppliers. Executives, managers, professionals, and practitioners at all levels—as well as consultants—will use it as a desktop reference.

Keywords

agility, business transition, capacity, cash flow, collaboration, executive team, holistic, improvement, integrated, operations strategy, partnerships, priority setting, speed, vision, business strategy

Contents

Foreword

While working with mid-sized companies and Fortune 500 firms across the globe, I can state unequivocally that the most successful organizations tether their operational management and practices thereof, firmly to their overall strategy.

Companies with sustained performance have a well-defined and articulated purpose—their why. From this they develop a strategy that reflects and responds to their customers' requirements and they willingly adapt their business practices as necessary to consistently meet customer expectations and to remain aligned to strategy.

This book guides business leaders in taking the steps to move their business into the "express lane." Even more importantly, it does so in a way that is simple and straightforward and recognizes and reflects the unique challenges of the mid-market. The models and the key learnings in each chapter provide the opportunity for solid understanding of the concepts and an excellent opportunity for shared learning among management teams.

I have had the great fortune of collaborating with Rick Pay over the past several years. He brings a practical, straightforward, and pragmatic approach to every situation. He draws upon his corporate experience and work with many presidents, CEOs, operations executives, and owners of mid-sized companies. I expect they relish his advice as it is easily understood and can be rapidly implemented.

We are facing unprecedented levels of disruption. For the past several decades, technology has been an enabler. We have access to more data about our customers, suppliers, competitors, and our own metrics than ever before. It is now enabling unforeseen levels of disruption—at the industry level, company level, and individual level. Consider Amazon's purchase of Whole Foods enabling one-stop ordering and home delivery, the eventual elimination of most call centers, bank teller, and truck driver jobs, and the destruction of traditional industry silos. The geopolitical environment has changed—Brexit, the election of Donald Trump, Spain's constitutional crisis over Catalonia, the potential demise of NAFTA, and changes to other global trade agreements. Tax reform is under consideration by world leaders and lobbied by constituents.

The aging population in developed countries and population growth in developing countries will place new demands on companies and countries that we have not yet considered. The demographic changes and other disruptors have already contributed to many mergers and sales of mid-sized companies.

Rick understands how owners can uncover the golden opportunities in their companies and retain a greater share of earnings. Rick's holistic approach, outlined in this new book, identifies ways to increase the valuation of one's firm.

Lorraine Moore
Strategic Advisor, Author, Speaker
Accelerate Success Group
Calgary, Alberta

Introduction

Rapidly increasing the value of your company benefits the stakeholders, whether you plan to transition or dramatically improve company performance. Many companies use approaches such as Lean, Six Sigma, theory of constraints, and others as their driving force for improvements. While these are useful tools for continuous improvement in today's business environment of innovative and disruptive change, these approaches no longer provide the differentiation needed to speed past the competition to higher levels of performance. Innovative, dramatic change comes from a holistic, integrated approach to business and operations strategy development. Business vision and operations strategy coupled together in tight alignment can take your business to levels of performance you have never imagined.

Many companies use the annual planning retreat as their tip of the hat to strategy development. But a CEO/owner-driven approach can provide much higher levels of growth, profitability, and cash flow. As part of developing this book, I interviewed six executives of successful companies to explore how they developed and aligned their business and operations strategies to achieve the company vision.

The companies and executives were:

- Lanz Cabinets—president, Brent Lanz
  Lanz Cabinets produces, delivers, and installs kitchen, bath, laundry, and pantry cabinets to single and multifamily housing in the western United States.
- Leupold & Stevens, Inc.—VP, manufacturing, Rob Nees
  Leupold designs and manufactures innovative optics for hunters and shooters.
- Pearson Packaging Systems—CEO, Michael Senske
  Pearson Packaging Systems specializes in the design, production, and integration of secondary packaging automation solutions.

- Pine Meadow Golf—Director, Bryan O'Doherty
  Pine Meadow Golf is part of a highly diversified
  conglomerate, made up of companies across a broad
  range of products.
- Nautilus—VP, operations, Chris Finley
  Nautilus is committed to helping people reach their fitness
  goals by providing strength and cardio equipment.
- Vigor Industrial—COO/CFO, Wayne Graham
  Vigor Industrial is a provider of shipbuilding, complex
  fabrication, and ship repair and conversion.

These companies represent a variety of industries and company sizes, but all are in the middle market, to which this book is most relevant. All of the companies are growing and are leaders in their markets. The variety in approaches to the planning processes provides an interesting backdrop to this book as do the commonalities in their methods. Who leads the process, who is involved in planning, the extent to which the process is strategy driven versus financially driven, the time the planning process takes, the measures of success, and other elements vary but seem to work for the companies. All recognized that their approach could be improved.

Partnerships, which I wrote about in my book, *1 + 1 = 100: Achieving Breakthrough Results Through Partnerships*, are essential to the strategy development process, using both vertical and horizontal partnerships in the organization. Alignment is the key to successful strategy development with the business strategy guiding development of the operations strategy, and the operations strategy informing the business strategy as to what is possible in terms of quality, delivery, cost, cash flow, and capacity.

But the key component is speed. Dr. Lisa Lang of the Science of Business consulting firm says that focusing on efficiency creates inefficiencies. She suggests flow should be the focus, especially in job shops. Taiichi Ohno of Toyota believed that speed was the element that most improved the business. Looking at speed helped identify the elements that, when removed or improved, would most dramatically improve performance. This book looks extensively at speed as the key to alignment and improvement of results.

I draw on my experience both as a VP, operations, of a rapidly growing middle market manufacturer and over 30 years of consulting, primarily in middle market companies. The approaches herein apply not only to manufacturers, but also to distributors, retailers, service companies, professional firms, and just about any type of business. I believe that aligning your business strategy and operations strategies in a holistic and integrated way will accelerate profitability and growth and move your company into the express lanes to rapidly increase company value and speed past your competition.

CHAPTER 1

Moving Fast

For companies to get into the express lanes and move to the next level of performance, they need to think differently as they develop both the business vision and strategy and operations strategy. Otherwise they are trying to outperform their competitors by doing the same things better, an effort that leads only to incremental improvement. To reach the top 10 percent, what I call world-class performance, companies need to innovate, using disruptive ideas to move to a new plane of performance. They need to not just think outside the box; they need to do away with the box. Using the power of speed, partnerships, and world-class thinking, companies can truly change the scenery.

Many small and middle market owners are considering business transitions, either to family members, their management team, or through a potential sale to private equity or strategic buyers. Perhaps the owners are simply looking for ways to dramatically boost performance even if there is no transition in sight. If the business value can be maximized, the owner's wealth is maximized as well, and the resulting healthy company provides a place to work for its employees, contributes to the community, and is a strong partner for its suppliers.

In some cases, I have found that owners, who were once tired of the pressures and problems in their business and wanted to "get out," changed their minds when the fun returned to the business by focusing on speed. The resulting improvements made it worthwhile to go to work again every day. Sometimes after this renewal of energy throughout the company, the owner prolonged his career by several years and achieved dramatic increases in the company's value.

By aligning the business vision and strategy with the operating strategies of the various elements of the business, owners can provide a bright future for their families and other stakeholders. Taking a holistic and integrated approach to strategy provides:

- Speed
- Cash flow
- Profitability
- Improved capacity
- Agility

By moving into the express lanes, the company can accelerate past its competitors, achieving its objectives faster.

What Is the Express Lane?

To move into the express lanes of business toward accelerated profit and growth, you need to develop a holistic view of the business by connecting the operations strategy and business vision and overall strategy. Many middle market company leaders focus too heavily on one or the other, forgetting that connecting the two creates the horsepower for success.

The corporate vision expresses what you are trying to achieve in the future and why. Many companies set visions that are too long, often in the 5- to 10-year range. A lot can change during that time frame, causing the effort to lose energy. A good time frame for vision is two to three years.

Slow and Steady Doesn't Change the Scenery

Many companies have developed a solid foundation through the years by having great ideas and doing things well. Owners are often involved at the ground level, especially in the beginning, and put in their own blood, sweat, and tears to build the company. Often they believe that, because it worked in the beginning, it will continue to work in the future. Marshall Goldsmith, the consummate management coach, developed the philosophy and wrote a book called *What Got You Here Won't Get You There*, which explains that you must constantly redevelop and innovate to accelerate your success.

Recently I received a survey from a marketing company seeking to find out how companies address performance improvement and risk mitigation, two subjects on the top of executive minds. As I reviewed it, two things jumped out:

1. Most of the issues in the survey were internal and did not involve customers, suppliers, the community, and other outside partners.
2. The ideas proposed as "leading edge" had to do with information, communication, tracking, improving current processes, and collaboration.

It was basically the same old, same old—the kinds of things that don't really change the scenery.

I meet many business owners through networking and referrals, and some say, "We're doing fine and don't need any help." In today's marketplace, that is a warning sign of possible future decline for those companies, as their competitors are often speeding forward in their own express lane and will soon pass them by.

Speed—The Key Competitive Factor

Sun Tzu wrote in *The Art of War* that taking advantage of opportunities using "extraordinary speed" is the crucial component of victory. If your business is agile, you can take advantage of opportunities as they present themselves, and of new ideas as you develop them or learn about them. Sun Tzu often explained that the one thing most esteemed is divine swiftness.

Even today, companies of all kinds—manufacturers, distributors, insurance, communications, professional services, and retail—see speed as the key to profitability and growth. Even in my business, management consulting, speed is of the essence. My mentor, Alan Weiss, often says that what the client wants is a quick result. The way for me to win the war is by quickly providing excellent service and high return on investment (ROI).

If a company can learn to do things fast, it can take even greater advantage of methods like Lean, Six Sigma, and world-class manufacturing. So many companies are using these methods that using them *quickly* to make dramatic improvements is now the way to excel. Taiichi Ohno, the architect of the Toyota Production System (TPS), suggests that TPS is not about cost reduction, but about speed.

Another factor in speed is agility, the ability to change quickly. For example, how quickly can you respond to changes in the sales forecast, changes in labor availability caused by sickness, weather events, or other crisis? I have always said that the key for operations is to keep sales in the critical path. Agility and speed make that possible.

Particularly in job shop manufacturing where each custom order is only filled once, speed becomes the differentiator. If a company can deliver a product more quickly than its competitor, it will win more business. At times, customers may even be willing to pay a bit more for quick turnaround.

During the 1980s and 1990s manufacturing went through a wave of offshoring generated by a quest for cost reduction, particularly labor costs. Many manufacturers followed the trend like lemmings heading for a cliff. Soon they found their order turnaround times were longer, due not only to increased shipping time, but also customs delays, order consolidation, and dock time waiting for ships. When companies started looking at the total cost of production, including shipping delays and risk, they began to nearshore or reshore production. According to a 2013 survey by Alix Partners of the biggest advantages expected from nearshoring, the second most commonly cited was improved time to market, in other words, speed.

Speed is one of the critical elements in creating alignment with customers. It includes:

- Time to market for new products
- Cycle time
- Order processing time
- Order lead times

Many companies have cut costs by anywhere from 30 to 60 percent by reducing lead times and increasing speed, which also improves responsiveness to change and customization.

How can you create more speed in your company?

1. Eliminate anything that isn't needed. Rather than just trying to work faster, assess the process and eliminate unnecessary steps. One way to do this is through process mapping and asking the questions, "Why do we do this?" and "Does this step provide value to the customer and would they pay for it?"

2. Simplify. Shorten setup and changeover times in production and distribution. Reduce materials handling and waiting. Reduce part count, number of suppliers, and product assortment. One of my clients cut maintenance technician time by 30 minutes per day by changing the way the technicians' vans were restocked. The result was over 60 hours per day of savings—15,000 hours per year. Not only did that reduce costs, but often the technicians could do an additional service call per day, which increased revenue as well.

3. Measure lead times, cycle times, and on-time delivery. These measures drive problem-solving efforts and increase speed. A manufacturing client improved its shipped-on-time from 24 to over 80 percent simply by measuring and posting the results for the staff to see. Knowing the score inspired staff to make quick changes, which dramatically improved results.

Remember to get good first, then get fast. Also, slow down to speed up! Speed is often sacrificed to rework and mistakes or using larger batches to try to be efficient.

Cash flow should also be driven by speed. Many growing companies outrun their capital sources and soon begin to suffer from lack of working capital to purchase materials, hire labor, and increase capacity to support their growth. Using speed to manage cash flow can be critical to a company's survival.

Cash provides the jet fuel for growth. One measure I like to use to accelerate cash flow is the cash-to-cash cycle. It is simply the time it takes from when you first spend a dollar on materials or labor, to the point when you get it back from a customer. The equation is days of inventory, plus days of accounts receivable (A/R), minus days of accounts payable (A/P). For companies that don't have inventory, the equation is A/R days minus A/P days.

My better clients have cash-to-cash cycles of 50 days or less. World-class companies often have cycles of less than 10 days, and really fast companies are actually negative—they use their customers' money to pay for materials and labor. In its heyday, Dell had a negative cash-to-cash cycle. It took credit cards for sales, had truly just-in-time inventory (less than three days on hand), and paid suppliers in 10 to 30 days.

Two additional things need to be in place to provide acceleration and growth: key performance measures and capacity. Most IT systems collect data related to accounting, but don't do a very good job of collecting the kinds of data that operations can use to fine-tune their organization and processes. The right key performance measures are designed to change behavior throughout the organization and accelerate growth. Some of the vital things to measure include customer service, such as shipped-on-time, productivity, margins, asset turns, lead times, cycle time, and other speed-related metrics.

One ongoing debate is how to measure productivity. Jack Welch once said that the only measure of productivity is units of output per unit of input. For example, the best measure of labor productivity is dollars shipped per labor dollar. Many companies measure revenue per hour, or revenue per head, but there are expensive and cheap hours and higher and lower cost heads. Measuring dollar for dollar is foundational to analyzing performance over time.

Capacity is the muscle needed to accelerate into the express lanes. I have seen many companies increase capacity by 40 percent without capital investment. This helps to really drop profit to the bottom line in the form of fixed cost leverage. Some companies use Lean tools to help, but lean can make you skinny without adding muscle. Focusing on flow, lead times, appropriate partnerships with suppliers, and speed can all dramatically improve capacity.

Using speed as the key measure can move you to new levels of success. By maximizing speed, ROI, agility, and capacity, when the captain of your ship calls for full speed ahead, your organization can respond.

Technology doesn't guarantee speed; in fact, relying less on technology can actually boost speed. Do you know of companies that have implemented enterprise resource planning (ERP) systems, only to realize they had to add people and transactions to make them work? Adding conveyor systems, barcoding systems, automated material handling, and other technologies often creates "monuments" that cannot be easily moved or changed as process improvement takes place.

I suggest to clients that they "eliminate, simplify, then automate" before introducing new technology. While technology can have a very positive impact, it must be properly implemented and that involves planning for it to support the vision and strategy of the company, not just as a cost reduction measure. In many cases, simplified and visual processes such as vendor-managed inventory (VMI) and Kanban can be equally or even more effective than automation.

In my book, *1 + 1 = 100: Achieving Breakthrough Results Through Partnerships*, I discuss partnerships with the community, particularly in terms of employing people with special needs. In many cases, these jobs could easily be automated, but the companies that use sheltered work-shops and other organizations to hire employees with disabilities on a temporary basis would rather provide work experiences than automate. Not only is this a true partnership with the community, but it also keeps the company agile.

In other cases, automation can save the company from potentially moving to a more favorable work environment. For example, many states are raising minimum wages, which often presents a significant cost chal-lenge to small and middle market companies, particularly those with tight margins such as the restaurant industry. Companies have to consider the impact on higher wage positions, and they have to justify the raises with the value the employees provide. The unintended consequences are that workers often get fewer hours, companies move to lower-cost states, and companies use automation to eliminate jobs. If you have been in fast-food restaurants recently that have kiosks for ordering, or if you have seen more automation for picking fruits and vegetables, you have seen the impact of these policies.

Don't Hit the Wall

Racecar drivers will tell you that your car goes where you are looking. If you look at the wall as you come around a corner, the result is typically quite bad! They will also tell you that their pit crews spend untold hours tuning the frame and making sure the wheels are aligned.

In business, if your operations strategy and business vision aren't aligned, the expressway to profit quickly becomes bumpy and you may slide into the wall. Taking a holistic, integrated view of the business and operations helps strike the essential balance between strategy (the *why*) and tactics (the *how*).

Owners who grew up in the company, usually in a technical role such as sales, engineering, or finance, run many small and middle market companies, and are more comfortable dealing with the day-to-day activities than developing strategy and looking to the future. Especially in companies that are financially driven, the focus on gross profit margins can blind the owners to greater opportunities. An overarching focus on Lean and Six Sigma to cut costs is a good indicator that company leaders are more invested in tactics than strategy.

Cost reduction techniques no longer provide an advantage because everyone uses them. In addition, an exclusive focus on cost reduction leads to practices like offshoring that don't provide the strategic advantage owners hope for, and can really slow the company down. Remember total quality management (TQM) in the 1980s? It was short-lived as a company focus because everyone became fixated on trying to do it right the first time.

Companies suffer when executives don't appreciate the return on time. When companies delay improvement, their competitors roar past in the express lane. Do any of these excuses sound familiar?

- It is busy season so we have to wait.
- We cannot afford the outside guidance from coaches or consultants, so we will wait until we have more discretionary funds.
- We will be hiring a new (insert position here), and need to wait until they are on board so they can lead or participate in the process.

One prospect I recently pursued delayed the start of an important project by six months while they hired a new VP, Operations. There was further delay while the new person got their feet on the ground. Then they discovered they had made a bad hire, so almost a year later the process started all over again.

How do you avoid hitting the wall of delay? First, have a clear road map of where you want to go, starting with vision and strategy. Vision drives change by defining the future state.

Next, set priorities. Many managers I talk to have very long to-do lists. I have found that, if they have more than three or four priorities, they really have no priorities. Everything is a crisis. Select the top three or four things and put the rest in the parking lot for the future. Using approaches like A, B, and C priorities don't work, because the B and C priorities will rarely if ever be addressed. It is better to focus on a few A items and leave all the rest on the future list.

The cost of doing nothing is very high. In some cases, just a few weeks head start can make all the difference between winning and losing. Companies like Amazon, Zara, Zappos, and others clearly understand the value of speed. Where does your company stand?

Key Learning

- Moving to the express lane increases company value.
- The key elements of the express lane are:
    - Speed
    - Cash flow
    - Profitability
    - Capacity
    - Agility
- Speed provides the innovative competitive advantage needed to move ahead of the competition.
- Align your operations strategy with the business vision so that you don't hit the wall.

CHAPTER 2

What Is Strategy?

Strategy, pure and simple, is the approach you intend to use to reach your vision. In his book, *Best-Laid Plans: Turning Strategy into Action Throughout Your Organization*,[1] Alan Weiss says there are two elements to strategy: what you want to achieve and how you intend to do it. This encompasses both the "what" and the "how" of strategy. Unfortunately, many companies fail to connect these two elements. For any strategy to be successful, there must be clear alignment between the vision, the business strategy, and the operations strategy.

We could also say that strategy is the framework that guides the choices that determine the organization's nature and direction.[2] Think of taking a trip. If you are going from Seattle to San Francisco, the vision (desired outcome) is to reach San Francisco on a particular date. The strategy includes whether to fly or drive. If you drive, do you take the freeway or go down the coast? As shown in Figure 2.1, there can be many alternative strategies that will move you from the current state toward your vision.

In business, strategy should be distilled into a brief statement, a couple of sentences that executive and management teams can communicate easily and clearly. Many companies conduct a two-day off-site retreat to develop strategy and produce a book about the results, which then typically sits on a shelf until the next retreat. Retreats can often do more harm than good. Often the executives that should be participating are looking at their e-mail and stepping out to make calls rather than engaging in the conversation. When they get back to the office, they commiserate

---

[1] 1994, Las Brisas Research Press.
[2] Tregoe, B., and J.W. Zimmerman. 1980. *Top Management Strategy; What It Is and How It Works,* 17. New York, NY: Simon and Schuster.

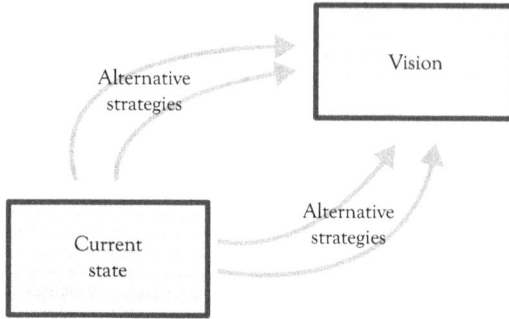

Figure 2.1 Operations strategy moves you from the current state toward the vision

with others about how useless it was, and sometimes valuable people even leave the company out of frustration over this waste of their time. Many retreats include "experiences" such as playing golf or riding zip lines, but does gliding over a canyon on a rope really create the mind-set needed to develop innovative strategy?

In a well-meaning effort not to allow the retreat syndrome to take over, some companies require their board or top management to create strategy in a vacuum. Even though it might be quick, this is not very effective, either. The executive team's engagement and ownership are essential so that they understand the "whys" of the process in order to create better operations strategy and implementation plans. Engagement in the process improves the likelihood of buy-in down to the lowest levels of the organization, as well as effective strategy implementation.

During my interviews with six executives to explore their approaches to business and operations strategy, it became clear that some companies drive strategy in a singular fashion, with just the CEO or CFO as the engine behind the effort. In too many cases, strategy is handed down from on high, like the Ten Commandments, and the executive team is expected to implement something they had little or no role in creating, leading to implementation failures.

In contrast, at the more successful companies, although the CEO was the owner of the strategy development process, the executive team was very engaged. We will discuss that more in Chapter 7, "You Aren't in This Alone."

It might surprise you to learn that many strategy experts consider the term "strategic planning" to be an oxymoron; in fact, Alan Weiss, who has been consulting in business strategy for many years, suggests there is simply no such thing as strategic planning, because planning is the activity that generates tactical methods to implement strategy rather than create it. By combining strategy creation with strategy implementation, a company may actually be setting the stage for failure by shifting the focus to tactics before the strategy is well-developed and aligned across the organization.

Operations strategy is the framework within which the company determines its ability to produce and/or deliver products and services to the customer, and takes cost, quality, speed, customization, and other elements that are essential within the context of the business strategy into account. Operations strategy involves structures, processes, and systems into which we will delve further in Chapter 4, "The Operations Strategy Puzzle." In small and middle market companies, the key is to provide frameworks that deliver results, growth, margins, customer retention and growth, and competitive advantage.

Vision

Vision is the driving force for the company. It answers the question, "Where are we going and why?" It provides the employees and other stakeholders with a more detailed understanding of their purpose and objectives than the mission statement (which is also important). A strong vision describes your ideal future to your employees and customers. In Lean terminology, it is the future state that you're trying to achieve in the next two to three years. The vision provides focus, sets clear goals, and provides a means for your people to set priorities. It tells them where and why, and should motivate people.

In his book *The Essence of Leadership: The Four Keys to Leading Successfully*,[3] Edwin Locke describes the vision as an image of the possible and desirable future state of the organization. He says that it must be realistic, credible, and attractive. In other words, it needs to energize the workforce to move toward the future.

---

[3] Lexington Books, 1991.

Jack Welch once said that the CEO's job is to create the vision and find the people to implement it. I believe it is also each executive's job to create a vision for their organization in support of the overall company vision. For instance, in the process of creating the operations strategy, there should be a related vision for operations that is aligned with the business vision. Where are we going, what do we want to achieve, and what will that look like?

Ideally, the vision should cover a period of 18 to 36 months. Shorter time frames do not allow enough to be accomplished, and longer ones don't tend to drive action since the future state is so far away (procrastination is always a danger), and they may be rendered invalid if the business landscape changes due to unforeseeable shifts in regulations, competitors, and disruptive ideas. While the mission can remain relevant forever, vision is finite.

When I was hired as VP, operations, for Supra Products, a company that made lockboxes for real estate agents, auto dealers, and other applications, the company's revenues were around $15 million and there was very little if any profit. The company president created a simple vision, which he called "55-15-5." He wanted to aim for $55 million in revenue with 15 percent profit before tax (PBT) in 5 years. He knew that would be a stretch, given that the company had existed for about 30 years and profits were elusive, but he thought we could make it and the executive team signed on, and in the end we hit his numbers almost exactly. We actually exceeded the PBT goal, reaching over 20 percent. When he created the vision, he didn't know that the company would dramatically change its revenue model, expand into China, and be sold to a private equity buyer, but the vision helped increase the company's value, and the president's family did well in the sale.

Supra's success aligned with Jack Welch's assertion that the CEO's job is to create the vision and find the people to implement it in two ways:

1. Supra developed a strong executive team of CEO, CFO, and VPs of operations, engineering, and sales who were completely on board with the president's vision.
2. The vision was succinct, and clear, ambitious, and attainable.

In addition, the company's executive compensation system helped us remain focused on the vision and the results we were trying to achieve. All of the executives stayed with the company through the change in ownership and continued its growth. A few years later, the buyer resold the company to a Fortune 500 for about five times what they paid for it.

Operations Strategy Options

Each of the operating departments should have their own strategy that aligns with and supports the company strategy. In this case, operations represents the delivery part of the business, often including supply chain, production, and warehousing/distribution, and possibly also customer service, IT, facilities, and other capacity-related services.

Innovation is crucial to operations strategy, and is the difference between excellent and average. Many middle market business executives are proud to tell me that they are meeting or beating industry average, but why not aim to be in the top 10 percent? When companies weave innovative thinking into the fabric of their operations strategy, they move beyond efficiency and do things differently.

Agility and flexibility are vital for innovation. Agility is the ability to change quickly, which enables managers to swiftly analyze, execute, and alter their strategy as needed to respond to market forces. Flexibility is the ability to bend without breaking, and a willingness to change while remaining focused on the company vision.

Agility and flexibility must precede continuous improvement, because revolutionary change, which occurs before continuous improvement, moves the company to a new plane, while the slower, evolutionary change of continuous improvement allows for small adjustments to existing processes. Agility and flexibly can move companies to world-class performance levels. At Supra, our vision for the supply chain was to get the right materials at the right time, in the right place, at the lowest possible cost. In the end, our PBT was over 20 percent and our inventory turns were 17, all while we shipped 99.8 percent on time. That is world-class performance.

Many companies focus on tactics without operations strategy. They might develop a strong business vision and strategy, but then they move right to approaches like Lean without putting them into the context of an

Holistic view
Corporate vision

	Strong	Weak
Strong	Accelerated profit and growth	Wandering in the wilderness
Weak	Can't keep promises	Death

Operations strategy

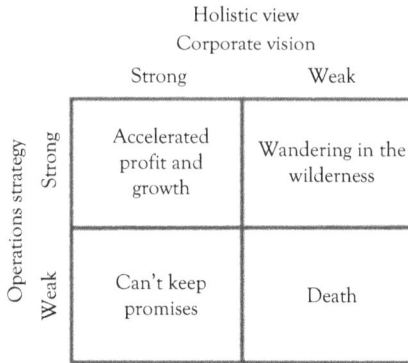

Figure 2.2 A holistic view of vision and strategy

operations strategy. Will Lean provide a competitive advantage, or simply keep the company on the same playing field as the competition? Trying to reduce costs without contextualizing the effort can undermine the results the company is trying to achieve.

A holistic view, one that balances business and operations strategy, links the operations strategy with the direction of the business and informs operational decisions. The CEO and other non-operations executives should get involved in developing operations strategy to maximize that alignment.

As shown in Figure 2.2, if you have strong corporate vision but weak operations strategy, you cannot keep your promises. If you have a strong operations strategy and weak vision, you are wandering in the wilderness. If both are weak, the company is dying. If both elements are strong, you are accelerating your profit and growth and dramatically increasing business value.

Let's look at Amazon as an example. For many years the company did not make a profit, but during that period, they were growing market share, developing their distribution model, expanding their product lines, and disrupting retail models that existed for decades. As it turns out, delivery/service is one of the five valid alternatives for operations strategy.

The Five Frames

There are five potential strategic frames for operations strategy. While many companies want them all, companies should choose only one (or possibly two) to drive the business. Trying to do all five often results in weak execution because there are too many priorities, and some frames are incompatible, for example, it may not be possible to offer high quality and low prices. Focusing on one primary and perhaps a secondary frame provides much stronger results. If you have more than two or three priorities, your efforts become diffuse and you accomplish very little.

The frames are:

- Low cost
- High quality
- Delivery/service
- Innovation
- Agility

Low Cost

Many manufacturers try to become the low-cost producer, which drives the ability to sell inexpensively and force their competitors out of business. Cost reduction often drives Lean initiatives, and at times purchasing will try to beat up their suppliers to reduce costs. Low-cost strategy frames drove many of the offshoring initiatives of the 1990s and early 2000s.

This strategy was extremely effective in Walmart's early days. Their business strategy was to be the low-cost alternative with a focus on small communities. Their operations strategy was to buy low-cost items (many of which were imported from China), and develop a distribution system that provided just-in-time delivery to their stores. Walmart became a driving force in the development of just-in-time (JIT) processes such as radio-frequency identification (RFID), which allowed them to know what was selling so that store inventory could be maintained. Cash management with high customer service levels provided a competitive advantage that was hard to match.

High Quality

Making the best product can be a very effective strategy, especially for markets driven by prestige or highly technical products. BMW, Mercedes,

Lexus, and other high-end carmakers developed high-quality strategies and used them to approach a high-priced market.

Interestingly, different carmakers define quality differently. In the case of Lexus, it is design. Remember the advertisement showing a ball bearing running down the hood/quarter panel seam? BMW defines quality in terms of the driving experience, and Mercedes defines it as leather and luxury. How quality manifests is quite different based on each company's business strategy.

Delivery/Service

Speed to market is also a key driver in operations. Short delivery cycles, quick manufacturing techniques, and high levels of service can drive competitiveness. Amazon, Dell, and FedEx all built highly successful companies using this driver.

Innovation

Companies that roll out innovative new products can drive their competitors crazy. The primary example of this is Apple.

Agility

The ability to quickly customize products also helps companies win market share. Toyota says it can deliver any car, customized to your liking, in 12 days or less.

For strategy to be useful, it has to provide the clarity and guidance that people need for decision making, and the five frames can prioritize activities in a way that supports your strategy.

Having alignment within your executive and management ranks is critical to success. During my business performance improvement projects, I ask executives and managers to rank the following four elements in terms of their importance to the company and its customers. Number one is most important and number four is least important, although still essential.

1. Cost
2. Delivery
3. Quality
4. Innovation

At one company, a manufacturer, where I asked five executives how their company ranked these four elements, I got four different answers. The reason I had been called in was their apparent inability to deliver products on time at a reasonable cost. Company profits were low, cash flow was a challenge, and morale was low. As I conducted my work, it quickly became apparent that misalignment among the management team was contributing to the poor performance, and the executives had no idea this misalignment was present. Unfortunately, this wasn't an unusual case.

Key Learning

- Operations strategy is the framework within which you design the company's key abilities to produce and/or deliver products and services to the customer.
- Strategy is what gets you to your vision.
- Vision is the driving force of the company. It describes your ideal future, two to three years out.
- The five frames for operations strategy are low cost, high quality, delivery and service, innovation, and agility.
- Alignment within your executive and management teams is vital for success.

CHAPTER 3

Taking a Holistic View

A holistic view of strategy creates a balance between the business strategy and the operations strategy. An integrated approach that addresses both simultaneously exploits core competencies, which can help the company achieve its vision. Many companies do the business strategy first, then the operations strategy. But by developing both strategies in an integrated fashion, they can contribute to each other.

In Figure 3.1, I show examples of organizations whose strategy is either clear or unclear, and whose tactics are effective or ineffective. Companies who have a clear strategy and effective tactics are the most successful.

The business strategy pulls the business ahead while the operations strategy synergistically pushes it. I call this Rick's Reciprocity Principle, and it functions like a freight train with engines in front that pull and additional engines in back that push. Many western rivers where I enjoy fly-fishing are neighbored by train tracks, with long freight trains running day and night. After noticing that those trains had locomotives at both ends, I learned that the combined push and pull greatly improves the trains' efficiency by reducing pressure on the couplings between the cars

	Strategy (what)	
	Strong	Weak
Strong (Tactics (how))	Clear strategy, effective tactics Microsoft, The Girl Scouts	Unclear strategy, but effective tactics U.S. auto industry, United Way
Weak (Tactics (how))	Clear strategy, but ineffective tactics Sears, The Red Cross	Unclear strategy and ineffective tactics United Airlines, The Boy Scouts

Figure 3.1 Balancing strategy and tactics

and on the wheels' interface with the track. The result is less wear, greater fuel efficiency, and a better-running train. Business strategy and operations strategy work together in much the same way.

For example, many companies are now looking at omni-channel distribution, which allows customers to order a product online or at stores and have their order shipped to them or pick it up at the store, as a better way to serve customers. If they order online and the product doesn't work out for them due to fit or other reasons, they can return it to a store, rather than shipping it back. Both Nordstrom and Macy's use this approach very effectively.

The ability to execute this approach is key in developing the business strategy, and including it in the company strategy helps drive the operations strategy as well. Developing and offering operations core competency can lead to stronger business strategies that accelerate profit and growth, so integrated holistic approaches can really drive the business toward its vision.

In privately held companies, these strategies should also take personal and family issues into account. What is the company's succession and transition plan? Are there things that need to be considered in the operations strategy to move toward a successful transition? Considering the changes needed for both transition and growth can have a major impact on the operations strategy, and can drive the business toward success.

Balancing Strategy and Tactics

Achieving balance between strategy and tactics is critical to success because of the demands on time at both the executive and mid-management levels. Making sure the strategies are in alignment reduces confusion and creates an environment where everyone is moving toward the same objectives. The top executives should focus on developing strategy and getting the right people on the bus through better hiring practices and by identifying people within the organization that can be moved into positions to implement it.

Both strategy and tactics exist to move the company toward its vision: a picture of the future state, as we saw in Chapter 2. Developing a balance between strategy and tactics improves business performance and increases value for your stakeholders.

Balancing strategy and tactics
Strategy

	Strong	Weak
Strong	Dynamic	Not prepared for the future
Weak	Not implemented	Chaos

Figure 3.2 The range of outcomes for companies in various states of strategy/tactics balance

Figure 3.2 shows the possible range of outcomes for companies in various states of strategy/tactics balance. Those that have strong strategy but weak tactics are unable to implement their strategy. Strong tactics and weak strategy leave a company unprepared for the future. If both strategy and tactics are weak, the company is in chaos; but if both are strong, the organization is dynamic, achieves word-class results, and dramatically improves value.

During my interviews of 6 middle market companies ranging in size from just under $30 million in revenue to over $600 million concerning how they align their business vision and operations strategy, it became clear that the more successful companies' leadership was heavily invested in strategy. Typically the CEO, president, or owner had a clear under-standing of the vision as well as the strategy that was driving the company. In several cases, CEOs spent 75 percent of their time (or more) focus-ing on the future, while their executive team developed tactical plans to implement the strategy.

At two of the companies, the CFO led the strategy development process and, not surprisingly, those strategies tended to revolve around financial results, performance improvement, capital planning, and risk reduction. The time frame tended to be shorter (12 to 18 months), and the planning process often began with a review of financial results and the more traditional strengths, weaknesses, opportunities, and threats analy-sis (SWOT), with focus on strengths and weaknesses.

In both cases, the operations strategy was weaker and tended to focus on initiatives, particularly those related to cost reduction. While the companies did have a strong financial performance, growth was slower than at the four companies where the CEO led the strategy development.

Two of the CEOs who drove the strategy development process focused on business development, market growth, new product development, and a strong corporate culture. One company's mission and vision were so strong that you could feel them when walking into the reception area and see them clearly on the website. This company "creates epic moments" for its customers in each of its three key markets. The board, family members (it is privately owned), and executive team all participate in the planning process, then each executive develops their strategy to implement and support the company strategy in their specific area.

Four of the six companies had very strong review processes. The company strategy implementation process was reviewed quarterly and gaps were identified for remedial action. In most cases, the operating strategies were reviewed monthly for gaps, and in one case the operating strategies were reviewed weekly. One might think that is too often and too granular, but strategy implementation is like flying to the moon; there are hundreds if not thousands of midcourse corrections required for a successful landing.

If you aren't looking at strategy, who is? If the executives focus on vision and strategy and let their key management team members handle the tactics, your company has the potential to delight your stakeholders beyond their expectations, and to "create epic moments" for your customers. Striking that balance between strategy and tactics will move you beyond the competition and prepare the way for a future state of value and success.

Getting Out of the Weeds

Some middle market company executives spend their day deep in the weeds of tactics. They think about strategy at the annual planning retreat, but the resulting five-year plan then sits quietly on the shelf in their office.

In the middle market, many CEOs and owner/executives started out in the tactical part of the business; they were originally salespeople, product developers, engineers, or technologists. They made their companies by directly contributing to growth. As their companies grew, however, they kept trying to contribute tactically while at the same time trying to steer the company through vision and talent development.

When executives stay in the weeds of tactics, two bad things happen. First, they don't get above the weeds to gain a strategic view of the marketplace. They are so involved in the day-to-day aspects of the business that they are not paying attention to the company's strategic direction. They are busy selling, designing, working with key suppliers, and so on, and no one is steering the ship.

Second, this can become very disempowering for the talent the CEO has brought on to help build the company. I have one client where the CEO asked me to improve shipped-on-time, profitability, and morale. As it turns out, part of the reason morale was bad was because the CEO randomly reduced labor hours in the bid process, which left the production floor unable to make products within budget. This in turn led to failure work because of attempts to build faster, which led to overtime, which reduced profit.

When to Start

If you have never had a business or operations strategy, the best time to start is now. If there has not been a business vision developed and in place, create one. It doesn't have to be perfect; you can always refine and update it as you go forward. If you do have one, review it to be sure it is up to date and in alignment with where you are now and where you want to go given the current state of your business, your markets, and your community.

Again, the vision should outline the desired outcomes and measureable goals for the next 18 to 36 months. It provides goals and context for the organization to use in the more detailed, operations-level planning.

The next step is to have an overall business strategy that defines the mission and objectives for the company as a whole. Part of this should be the business model, which defines how you make money. Developing the business model has many benefits, one of which is confirming that the company's activities actually yield the profit and cash flow needed to continue to grow and thrive. Many companies discover that their model either doesn't work, or worked at one time, but changing market conditions or the entry of disruptive competitors has rendered it ineffective. Failing to respond to changes that impact the business model can lead to the death of the business.

Each of the six companies I interviewed for this book has an annual planning process loosely tied to the company's fiscal year, which (for all six) ends on December 31, but that was where the commonality ended.

One company started its annual planning process in July, and another started in October. Two others waited until December and occasionally found that the process extended into the new fiscal year. The key is to start. Also important is making time before the fiscal year starts to seriously consider your plans and the budgets needed to implement them.

I find that many companies do not create annual budgets, and when they do the budget is created by the finance department, often with minimal inputs from the departments it impacts. The budget is frequently created and handed out as the marching orders to be followed with no buy-in. In many cases, it isn't followed and then executives wonder why the company is missing its profit targets.

I suggest you need to budget for profit. Budgeting for profit uses a direct cost/contribution margin approach in which variable and fixed costs are budgeted on their own, with specific attention to the profit margin and dollars you want to make. The model looks like this:

- Total revenue is based on unit volumes times revenue per unit
- Less direct variable costs: variable cost of sales + materials + variable direct labor + variable cost to produce/distribute
- Equals contribution margin
- Less targeted profit
- Equals the amount available for overhead

Too many companies leave profit to the last step, and often there is nothing left for profit. They then make seemingly random cuts that actually hinder the company's ability to provide quality products, on time, at the lowest possible cost. Morale often suffers as a result.

Overheads need to be budgeted in detail by department. Variable costs are managed as a percent of sales and fixed costs are managed to the budget. I have seen companies that use this model to produce pro forma financial results during the month to find out where they stand, rather than waiting for month end close, which can take 10 to 20 days after month end.

In addition to financial budgets that support the business and operations strategy, companies should also produce capital budgets and asset budgets, such as inventory and other cash flow-related items. This not only highlights these issues, but also provides a more holistic view of the company's financial and operating performance.

Setting the bar high in these areas leads companies to think differently about how they do things. They don't just try to get better; they improve exponentially by applying innovative approaches to their business. When Alaska Communications decided to reduce their inventory by over 200 percent, they couldn't just buy better to achieve the desired result, but they had to completely overhaul their approach to supply chain management. They developed partnerships with suppliers so that in some cases they didn't even touch the inventory or store it in their warehouses. The supplier partners provided true just-in-time delivery to construction sites and technicians, which helped reduce inventory levels from over $17 million to under $5 million.

The most successful companies I interviewed planned on an ongoing basis. They refined their plans continuously, measured results weekly or even daily, and set the bar high for performance. One unexpected thing I noticed at these companies was the pride in performance that permeated the organization, and the high morale that accompanied it.

The One Thing that Really Drives Success

Over the years I have helped many clients develop and implement innovative operations and supply chain strategy. One thing seems to make all the difference in their success: key managers who have the passion to get things done. As we have already seen, the foundation for strategy is to have the passion and participation of the company's leadership, especially the CEO, but real success is driven by the ability to implement the strategy. Too many strategies sit on the shelf until the next year, when executives discover that they didn't accomplish what they had planned.

Alaska Communications had a strong mid-level manager, the director, supply chain, who was assigned to implement their supply chain strategy, which the CFO had retained me to help develop. We had an advisory relationship, which means the director and I discussed implementation during regular phone calls and when I visited the company headquarters. We discussed supplier partnerships, JIT inventory management, Lean principles, team development, leadership, accountability, and many other topics. I soon noticed that, on one trip, we would talk about an issue, and the next time I visited he was taking me by the arm to show me what they had done and the amazing results they were achieving. I often asked myself, "Why is this client so successful when others aren't?" The main reason was they had the right people on the bus: people who drive change and have a passion for the ideas we developed to improve operations.

That one factor, a strong mid-management-level leader, is critical for success. In addition, three other factors are important:

1. Innovative thinking creating a vision for success
2. Having the right people in place throughout the organization, who participate in and support change
3. Developing partnerships both inside and outside the organization

The right people will not allow roadblocks to impede their progress; they see issues early and respond to them quickly. Having a strong middle-level manager that leads the charge in each key area of the company is critical to success in strategy implementation.

Key Learning

- Having a holistic and integrated view of the business strategy and operations strategy helps the company achieve its vision.
- There must be a good balance between strategy and tactics. Top executives should focus on strategy and let their next-level reports focus on tactics, within the boundaries set by the strategy.

- It is hard for mid-market leaders to get out of the tactical weeds because of their backgrounds in starting and initially growing their companies. It is difficult for them to switch to the strategic view as the company accelerates its profit and growth.
- One thing that really drives success in implementation is the presence of a strong mid-level manager who drives the day-to-day activity in pursuit of the operations strategy.

CHAPTER 4

The Operations Strategy Puzzle

When many companies develop an operations strategy, they focus on a few areas such as supply chain, labor, capacity, and perhaps some improvement methods such as Lean or Six Sigma, all of which are internally or upstream-focused and often related to cost reduction. There is much more to operations planning than that. It is more like a complicated jigsaw puzzle with interlocking pieces; if any one of them is missing, it leaves an obvious hole in the picture. Completing the puzzle with your colleagues can be fun, develop strong teams and relationships, and provide a great sense of accomplishment.

On the one hand, planning is never done. As the Nike slogan says, there is no finish line, because things keep changing—products, customers, sales channels, competitive factors, technology, and more, which means you need to continuously review your plans to improve them for the future.

Because change is a constant, I discourage companies from generating the classic 5- to 10-year plan, and strongly believe an operations plan should be focused on three years. Too often, either companies develop a plan that languishes on a shelf, or they stick with their plan for too long when key factors have changed or new competitive factors, such as disruptive technology, have emerged.

There are 12 key elements to operations planning, as shown as follows (Figure 4.1):

1. Management
2. Workforce
3. Supplier partnerships
4. Vertical integration
5. Supply chain
6. Business processes

Operations strategy elements

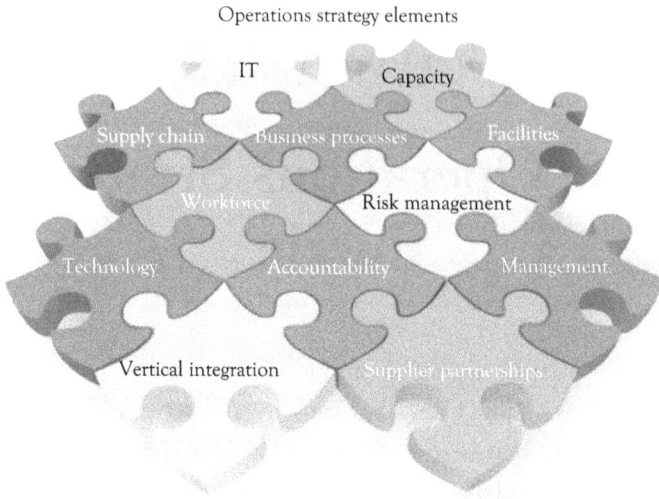

Figure 4.1 the elements of operations strategy

7. Capacity
8. Accountability
9. Risk management
10. Facilities
11. IT
12. Technology

These can be classified into three categories: people-related, process-related, and support and infrastructure.

People-Related

Many companies focus on direct labor as they plan their operations. While direct labor is certainly part of the strategy puzzle, there are a number of other people-related puzzle pieces that are just as important.

Management

I believe that one of the most important components to successful execution of the operations strategy is the operations management team. Many change initiatives fall apart at the middle management level because there are too many priorities, the pressure of day-to-day activities is overwhelming, or there are weak players on the team. These obstacles to carrying out implementation are described in the following Figure 4.2 as "Operating Beliefs," with the dissolution of the strategic directive shown as "Refraction."

The executive team, owner, or CEO of the company sets the vision for change, but as the plans go to management their lack of follow-through causes what we call refraction, causing change to stop in its tracks. When initiatives aren't carried out, everyone gets frustrated.

It is important to have the right people in the right positions to successfully carry out the strategy. With one of my clients, Alaska Communications, we undertook a significant strategic effort to reduce warehouse costs, reduce inventory, and improve morale. The supply chain director played a critical role not only in leading the change, but also in developing and supporting his workforce to get things done. His enthusiasm for the project was largely responsible for its success.

As Collins says in *Good to Great*, you have to have the right people on the bus, which also means having the right people in the right positions. Part of the strategy development process is to identify the management structure necessary to attain the organization's objectives. For example, if a strategic initiative is to develop supplier partnerships and increase use of

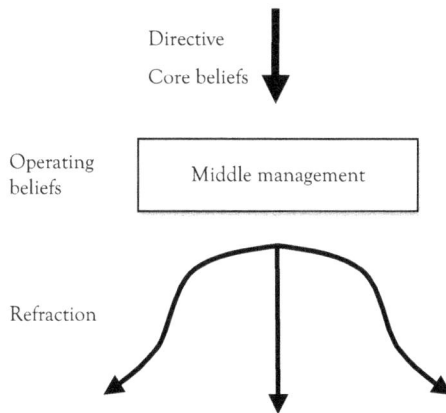

Figure 4.2 Obstacles to carrying out implementation

Source: Alan Weiss, Summit Consulting

auto-replenishment systems, you'll need a supplier business manager. This position is much more than just a buyer; it's the person who spends most of their time developing supplier relationships, holding suppliers accountable for results, working with other departments (e.g., sales) to develop plans, and putting in a lot of face time at both the company and the suppliers.

The supplier business manager's key responsibilities are:

- Developing and executing the supplier partner program
- Minimizing inventory while minimizing shortages
- Consolidating supplier base to reduce costs and improve quality
- Providing feedback to suppliers
- Monitoring forecasts for commodities
- Implementing auto-replenishment systems such as Kanban and vendor-managed inventory (VMI)
- Monitoring industry and commodity issues for supplier benchmarking and contingency planning

Workforce

The workforce is the foundation of operations and requires planning for the skills required and the number of people needed to produce, assemble, and ship the company's products or services. Many companies stop at that, but remember that, in the short run, direct labor behaves like a fixed cost; so on a month-to-month basis, as revenue cycles go up and down, companies will likely not release employees only to bring them back a month or two later in an attempt to control costs during those cycles. Therefore, direct labor costs tend to behave in a fixed way.

Fixed costs should be transformed into variable ones (costs that vary in direct relationship to revenue), and with labor that can be done via temps and overtime. Temporary workers can be released and brought back as revenue goes up and down, but need to be managed carefully in order to maintain quality and provide trained labor for operations, which can be done through partnerships with temporary labor service companies. I will discuss this further in Chapter 6.

Overtime works in a similar way. I always liked to use overtime as the first means for variable cost management since the benefit of overtime was that our employees earned more income. We almost always made a request for those willing to work overtime and only in limited cases had to require it. It was a win/win for the company and the employees. However, if the employees could not work the extra hours, we used temps.

I also found that hourly wages get employees, but benefits keep them. We tried to always pay just above the market average for the cities we were in, and then developed strong benefits packages, which many competitors for labor could not compete with. For example, not only did we have a generous 401(k) matching program, but we also sweetened the deal with profit sharing at the end of the year. In addition, we offered a generous vacation and sick time program as well as educational benefits. We required minimal vesting for these, because we felt that people who contributed to our success should enjoy the benefits from that success, regardless of how long they had worked for us. We did require that they be employed by us on the last day of the year to participate in any profit sharing. All of this was carefully budgeted and fit well within our performance goals for the company.

Finally, employee performance should be measured by productivity, and, as Jack Welch once said, that should be units of input per units of output, or dollars shipped per labor dollar. Many companies measure based on hours or head count, but hours can be either cheap or expensive, as can head count. Dollars to dollars is the only pure measure, and it should be managed based on a trend. You should also watch labor as a percent of revenue (again, dollars to dollars). At my prior company, as we implemented world-class manufacturing, labor went from 13 percent of sales to only 3 percent of sales overall, dropping 10 percent of sales to the bottom line over a five-year period, which was a world-class productivity improvement.

Supplier Partnerships

In operations planning, suppliers fall into the people-related category, and from a planning perspective they behave much the same as your internal teams, and can even play a role on internal teams. Supplier partnerships are founded on relationship and trust, and require strong communication of expectations and performance, like direct labor. Supplier partnerships ensure that your company gets supplies at the lowest possible cost, at the highest possible quality, on time. When communication is strong, everyone knows what is expected and how they are doing. More on this is available in my book, *1 + 1 = 100: Achieving Breakthrough Results Through Partnerships*.

The planning process should cover the kinds of suppliers needed, what capabilities they should have, how they will be managed (see supplier business manager), and what new relationships will need to be developed because of other elements of the plan, such as geographic growth, new product support, or commodity market changes. In addition, some suppliers enthusiastically support auto-replenishment systems and others don't; so if your plan calls for increased use of Kanban, VMI, or other auto-replenishment processes, you may need to change suppliers.

Process-Related

Vertical Integration

Vertical Integration is arguably the foundational element of operations strategy. The classic "make versus buy" question sets the stage for additional planning for labor, materials, facilities, IT, and most of the rest of the puzzle pieces. Unfortunately, most companies make this decision based on simple cost–benefit analysis. A total cost of ownership (TCO) view is needed to properly assess whether the company should develop the resources to build, or manage outside suppliers.

TCO takes a broad perspective on costs. The classic TCO model looks at components of cost upstream, inside, and downstream from the company, or, in other words, pre-transaction, transaction, and post-transaction costs.

Pre-transaction costs include:

- Engineering and design
- Materials requirements
- Supplier sourcing
- Tooling
- Contracting
- Adapting systems
- Ordering processes, including auto-replenishment

Transaction costs include:

- Item price
- Order placement
- Pipeline costs
- Receiving
- Quality and inspection
- Return of parts
- Scrap
- Order-related issue resolution
- Payment

Post-transaction costs include:

- Production and warehouse fallout
- Field failures
- Repair and replacement costs
- Repair parts requirements
- Cost of materials disposal
- Obsolescence
- Cost of holding inventory

Many outsourcing decisions could be reversed once companies view them from a TCO perspective. If TCO had been used when many companies went to China for production in the 1990s, I suspect the tide may have turned.

Supply Chain

Planning for supply chain is quite complex, and many books have been written on this subject. Supplier selection and management, inventory management, logistics, quality issues, speed (lead times and cycle times), auto-replenishment systems, geographic dispersion, and more could be applied to this piece of the operations strategy puzzle. When planning for operations strategy, supply chain can be a significant competitive weapon, and how fast items can be delivered can become the competitive factor in company success, as shown by Zara, Wal-Mart, Amazon, and many others.

Business Processes

When considering operations strategy, whether to add, strengthen, replace, eliminate, or automate becomes key in long-term decision making. Some examples of the business processes to consider include:

- Order processing
- Scheduling
    o Production
    o Labor
    o Materials flow
    o Plant and warehouse
- Inventory management and control
- Quality
- Safety
- Cost accounting
- Supplier selection
- Key performance measures
- Lean/Six Sigma/Theory of Constraints/Theory of Delays
- Levels of authority
- Labor management

Some would suggest that the quality and power of your business processes make all the difference as competitive factors. I believe that part of operations discipline is the strength of your processes, and whether the employees understand them and are held accountable for using them.

Capacity

While capacity could be seen as an infrastructure issue, I believe that business processes drive many elements of capacity. Capacity is related not only to production and warehouse processes, but also to people, suppliers, buildings, and supply chains. Consider capacity to be related to the various pipe sizes that drive the company's ability to produce and deliver its products or services from the supplier's supplier to the customer and often to the customer's customer. People, processes, facilities, and more can impact that ability, and capacity size (and the ability to quickly change that size) relates to capacity planning in the broader sense of the word.

For example, in my prior position as VP, operations, we had an opportunity to take a large chunk of business from our competitor if we could flex rapidly both up and down. The VP, sales, came into my office one day and announced that our chief competitor had a massive field failure of their product, and, if we could double our output for about 120 days, we might force the competitor out of business. I told him I would get back to him the next day with my answer.

We knew that this was a one-time deal and that we did not need to plan for ongoing operations at this level of performance, but at the same time we assumed our capacity was 25,000 units per month and we were being asked to go to 45,000 units. We called the effort "Project 45." I pulled my team together and we considered the following, making calls and pulling people into the meeting for input:

- Could our production lines double their capacity?
- Did we have the labor capacity to do the work, including willingness of people to work overtime (it was nearing the holiday season)? Could we quickly get temporary workers of sufficient quality to help?
- Could our suppliers respond quickly in terms of parts and capacity?
- Could our warehouse operations support the increased flow of materials?
- Could our quality inspectors keep up with the statistical-based inspections we used?
- Did we have the ability to stage product for shipment?
- Could our logistics providers respond rapidly?
- Could we set up multi-shift operations, including the support mechanisms such as cafeteria services?

The bottom line was that we not only succeeded in hitting 45,000 units per month, but we actually made it to 60,000 units. Our production surge damaged the competitor to such an extent that they ultimately went out of business.

One thing we learned was that our capacity was not 25,000 units, as we'd previously believed. It was also not 60,000, but somewhere in between. We also learned that we could be very agile because our planning process and business processes were robust.

Accountability

Behavior and accountability help drive operations discipline. The behavior you want to instill in your organization is to follow the process and continuously look for improvement opportunities. To do this, people need to know what is expected and how they are doing, which requires measurement and reporting.

In order to drive accountability, reporting needs to show the trend over time. In many cases, reporting to budget or reporting compared to last month or last year may not be relevant to the current situation. Performance to plan is better, but that assumes you have a good plan. I like to show the trend of performance in order to answer the simple question, "Are we getting better?"

The easiest way to show that is a graph with a trend line, as we see in Figure 4.3.

This chart shows operating expenses for a small manufacturing company by month. Sometimes, because of performance variability (such as the month-to-month variations in Figure 4.3), it is hard to tell if things are getting better or worse. In this case the trend line is going down significantly over the course of the year, indicating that costs are declining, which is good.

These kinds of charts need to be posted in places where the appropriate people can see them, which normally means on the shop floor, in the warehouse, in the office, or outside the lunchroom (one of my favorite places).

In addition, people need to know that the charts are important to look at and understand. When we first started posting performance boards at the manufacturer where I worked, I asked the CEO to come

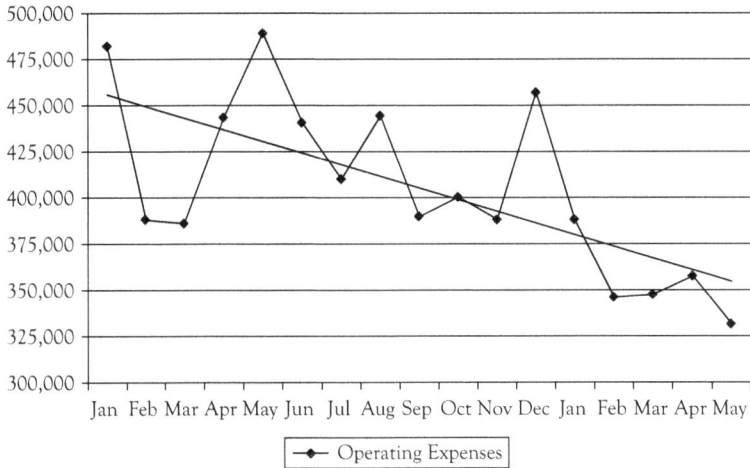

Figure 4.3 Showing trends over time

out occasionally and look at them, pondering each chart. Not only did people see him doing this, but occasionally he would go get someone and ask him or her about one of the charts, which had a huge impact; people didn't want to be asked by the CEO and not know what the chart meant. In addition, we held our stand-up meetings by the charts for each work center, discussed what they said, and asked for input on improvement. Then, most importantly, we took action on the suggestions.

Risk Management

This topic could fall under the next category, but I think it is a process within itself and needs to be considered as such. To manage risk, we must ask what could go wrong, how are we going to prevent that, and, if it happens, what will we do? Many companies ask the first and last questions, but fail to consider prevention.

There are two kinds of action, preventive and contingent. If the fire has started, you put it out (contingent action). To do so quickly, you install fire extinguishers or sprinkler systems, but those are also contingent actions, because you use them only after the fire has started. Preventive action asks the question, how do we avoid having a fire in the first place? That might include education programs, allowing smoking only in designated areas and with appropriate cigarette butt disposal, fire marshal inspections, safety programs, and audits.

When planning for operations, it is important to consider what kinds of risks may occur, what we can do to prevent them, and what to do if they happen. I had one client that had not considered this, had a fire in the building, and had no way to quickly contact all of the employees to tell them not to come to work.

Some examples of the kinds of risk to consider include:

- Supply chain interruptions
- Late deliveries
- Employee disruptions such as widespread sickness or labor strife
- Facility damage due to fire, flood, or extreme weather
- Quality shutdown such as food-borne problems
- Government and regulatory issues
- Lack of skilled labor to support fast growth
- Machine downtime

All of these should be built into a matrix in your plan showing both the preventive and contingent actions, along with the one person accountable (the person who owns the risk response).

Support/Infrastructure

Facilities

Obviously, planning for facilities is important for two reasons: (1) they consume a lot of capital and (2) it can take a while to build, remodel, and adjust them to respond to capacity needs (more on that later). But facilities can play other large roles in the company's performance.

One overlooked aspect is the impact facility design has on internal communications and morale (e.g., when Supra Products built a new 120,000-square foot manufacturing facility). The entire production part of the building was separated from the offices (sales, customer service, accounting, HR, and executives) by a large hallway that ran all the way from one side of the building to the other. You might as well have put the two sides of the building in separate states. Rarely did the production people go to the offices and the office people hardly ever went into production. Class warfare erupted and communications and morale suffered. Management immediately responded with a few simple approaches that really helped the situation. First, the executives made it a point to walk through production whenever they were going to a meeting. They would observe, chat with workers, look at performance charts, and generally be seen, which production employees really appreciated. Second, employee meetings were held semi-monthly in the lunchroom to improve communications and the spirit of teamwork.

I have seen parking lots, walls, building campuses, and other well-meaning building designs create similar problems, which strong facilities planning would help alleviate.

Other facilities planning issues include size, location, and function. Often, the smallest thing can interrupt productivity and service. In one building, the location of the copy center disrupted paper flow and prevented people from getting documentation developed, produced, and shipped on time. In another, the location and design of the mail room caused hours of productivity loss. Again, a little forethought can save a lot.

IT

IT can be one of those resources that are both a blessing and a curse. The blessing is that strong IT can improve communication and order processing, provide on- and in-line resources such as work instructions at the point of work, and more. It can be problematic because it can be inflexible and creates a "monument" that gets in the way of continuous improvement.

IT systems need to be subservient to operations needs, not drivers of how things are done. While it is important that people be willing to meet the system partway, IT often seems to harm as much as it helps. In my prior job, we implemented a system that required an extra inventory transaction for every item, which required us to hire three more people. One of the goals of the system was labor savings, so we started out in the hole.

Technology

More than IT, technology encompasses things like robotics, bar code systems, communications systems such as handheld radios, lift trucks, automated material handling systems, and more. While much of this might be under the IT department's control, these types of technology need to be addressed specifically in the operations plan. When companies pay attention to the cost benefit and value the technology provides, it can promote continuous improvement rather than becoming a monument that hinders progress.

Key Learning

There are 12 elements to operations strategy, and together they form what I call the operations strategy puzzle: a clear picture of the framework necessary to attain the business vision. The 12 elements are:

1. Management
2. Workforce
3. Supplier partnerships
4. Vertical integration
5. Supply chain
6. Business processes
7. Capacity
8. Accountability
9. Risk management
10. Facilities
11. IT
12. Technology

The strategy should focus ideally on three years to acknowledge the possibility and impact of change. Focusing on all 12 elements helps management to see the entire battlefield and not get caught up in a few skirmishes, such as Lean and cost reduction.

CHAPTER 5

Components of Value

The term "value" is often associated with businesses that are in transition, usually through a sale, but improving value can drive performance improvement even when there is no plan for a sale, or if the potential sale is three to five years in the future. I have worked with some business owners who no longer enjoyed running their companies because of challenging circumstances, family issues, or just plain boredom; but when improving the company's value led to significant performance improvement, the fun returned and they decided not to sell after all.

When owners do plan to sell, they find that buyers come in two types, strategic and financial, who are looking for different things but whose ultimate objective is to increase the value of the company or combined entity.

What Do Company Buyers Buy?

When I was VP, operations of Supra Products, a rapidly growing manufacturer, a family of entrepreneurs owned us. The father had started the company and ran it for almost 30 years, and over time his two sons became involved in the business. Some typical family issues emerged, and they decided to sell the company. Several potential buyers showed interest, and the owners eventually entered into due diligence with a group of family trusts from the eastern United States. This was the classic financial buyer.

The due diligence process focused primarily on the company's current and future financial performance, while also exploring future revenue growth opportunities through new products, new markets, expanded current markets, and changes to the way things were sold. For example, our CFO created the means to lease the product to the market as well as selling it, which generated an ongoing stream of revenue, in addition to the onetime revenue source from sales.

I asked Supra's buyers what they were looking for in the many small and middle market companies they bought, and they listed three things:

1. Revenue growth
2. Profit growth
3. Projected future cash flows

At first I thought, "That's it?" But then it occurred to me that financial buyers are very likely to resell the company in the future, and their three priorities drive the high valuation they are looking for. Financial buyers are interested in a company's potential future value, rather than its current value, which is what many executives focus on.

Strategic buyers, on the other hand, are looking for synergies in the business strategy, such as:

- Market growth
- Expanded product offerings
- New technology
- New talent
- Expanded customer lists
- Opening of new geography
- Increased capacity

Like financial buyers, they look for revenue growth, profit growth, and projected future cash flows, as well as innovation and a strong management team.

Innovative companies create new products and new markets. Strategic buyers are looking for strong product development and creativity in product design, perhaps more than financial buyers. For example, when Hershey bought Krave, the jerky producer, they were looking to expand in the snack food industry. Krave was very creative in building new markets, having recently expanded into women's and postexercise markets by developing new flavors and new packaging. Hershey paid a higher price for Krave than the industry had ever seen; clearly Hershey valued innovation.

Strategic buyers may also be looking for a strong management team, particularly one with expertise in areas in which the buyer wants to improve, such as Lean techniques and supplier partnerships. Alaska Communications in Anchorage embarked on a yearlong process to improve inventory and service levels at their retail stores by developing auto-replenishment systems to help ensure the right amount of inventory was on hand, while maintaining high customer service levels. The system was so effective that the improved revenue and reputation helped lead to the successful sale of the wireless division to a strategic buyer.

Increasing Value

When owners and executives decide to rapidly increase their companies' value, they should consider three areas:

1. Vision
2. Holistic strategy
3. Performance improvement

The vision is the target state of strategic planning, and should be limited to three years into the future. Many companies craft 5- and even 10-year visions, but so much can change over that amount of time that I believe three years is the best boundary for believable, actionable visions. The vision is critical to change initiatives because not only does it define the future state, but it helps explain why the change is occurring. To be invested in change, employees need to understand why.

A holistic strategy is a combination of the business strategy and the operations strategy, which creates the reciprocal effect I outlined in Chapter 3. Using our train engine metaphor, the pullers in front are like the business strategy and vision, while the pushers in back are like the operations strategy. This push/pull effect has very positive results.

In business, aligning the operations strategy with the business strategy accelerates profit and growth, which increases company value, as shown in Figure 5.1.

Rick's reciprocity principle

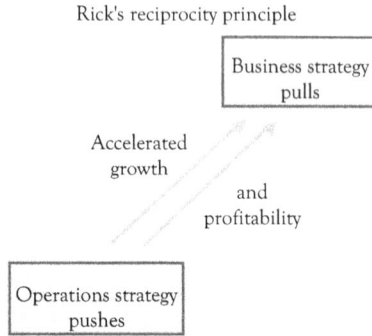

Figure 5.1 Operations strategy drives growth and profitability

The third thing that strategic buyers look for in a company is performance improvement. Buyers are looking for ways to quickly increase the value of their investment so they can potentially sell it at a later date for a significant multiple of what they paid for it. Recent performance improvements are often discounted unless they have been in place for several years and show a strong trend of continuing improvements. Buyers also look for potential improvements they can exploit after the acquisition is complete; improvements in cash flow and profitability in particular can be very attractive. One example would be the ability to rapidly improve inventory turns to free up cash to help pay any acquisition costs.

When companies want to grow, become more profitable, or increase cash flow, how can executives or potential buyers assess operational readiness for improvement? For example, how do they know if deliveries can be made on time or that the company's current suppliers can keep up with the growth?

I've developed the Performance Command Center, a system of measuring a company's readiness to increase its value. Picture the dashboard of a small aircraft. In the middle is a big dial called the artificial horizon—arguably the most important dial on the dash—that tells the pilot if the plane is going up or down, is turning left or right, or is upside down. In the Performance Command Center, that dial is speed, as shown in Figure 5.2.

Speed includes lead times, cycle times, shipped-on-time, product development life cycles, and so on. Many companies, like Amazon and

Figure 5.2 The performance command center

Zara, use speed as their significant competitive advantage. Amazon has grown dramatically not only by expanding their online product offerings, but by delivering rapidly to consumers, often in creative ways, like offering secure package retrieval from yellow Amazon Lockers, developing their own Uber-like fleet of delivery drivers, and planning trial runs of a drone delivery system. Zara, the Spanish clothier, can take high fashion women's clothing from the designer's desk to the store in as little as two weeks by having very short, fast supply chains.

In addition to speed, the Performance Command Center uses profit, cash flow, capacity and agility, and additional measurable components of company value (or potential value). Profit and cash flow almost go without saying, but I will mention that even profitable companies can end up in trouble when they don't manage their cash flow. Any commercial lender will tell you that many of the companies that end up in special assets are there because of cash flow problems, not necessarily lack of profitability.

Capacity is much more than capital equipment; it is the ability to balance the company's growth goals. Capacity includes suppliers, maintenance and support, distribution, and labor. As an example, many of my clients have trouble finding skilled workers to help grow the company, such as machine operators and maintenance technicians. Many of our schools today encourage students to plan for college, rather than encouraging some to go to trade schools to learn how to run CNC machines, and this has created a large gap in skilled labor.

I recently toured a machine shop and noticed that almost all of the operators and maintenance technicians appeared to be in their 60s and 70s. I asked the CEO, who was giving me the tour, if he was concerned about that, and he replied that he was scared to death. As the older workers retire, they will leave a large hole in his workforce that he knows will be difficult to fill, and the scarcity of skilled workers impacts his company's capacity.

Agility is the ability to change rapidly, anywhere in the organization and even in the supply chain. Many companies don't handle change well. I spoke with a CEO and his team about performance improvement, and their biggest concern was how to engage in the improvement efforts when they were already swamped with the company's day-to-day needs. This issue is most evident at the middle management level, where managers are responsible not only for maintaining the performance standard for current orders, but also for leading improvement efforts. This conflict can lead to substandard results in both areas.

Attending to all five elements of the Performance Command Center can yield major improvements that dramatically drive up the company's value.

Destroying the Box

To dramatically increase a company's value, you can't just think outside the box, you have to destroy the box. Many executives have (intentionally or not) created artificial boundaries for their company's growth by limiting themselves to the way things have always been done, or through incremental, short-lived improvements through programs such as Lean, Six Sigma, or Theory of Constraints. The way to achieve dramatic improvements of 20 to 40 percent (and more) is through innovation and disruptive ideas, like Amazon and Zara.

One route to innovation is through partnerships. Many companies collaborate, but true partnerships can provide results beyond the scope of incremental improvement. For example, in their effort to improve warehouse performance, Alaska Communications (ACS) turned operations over to the customers and boosted productivity by 75 percent. Here's how they did it.

During the short summer construction season in Alaska, crews often work 20 hours per day, and sometimes around the clock, but ACS's warehouse was open only 40 hours per week, causing expensive delays when crews couldn't access the materials they needed. Because ACS had complete knowledge and control over what flowed into and out of the warehouse, they could turn operations over to the customers and let them have 24/7 access to materials. Using spot cycle counts, ACS had strong internal controls, which the accounting team accepted. The customers were happy and ACS achieved a 75 percent productivity improvement as a result, a great example of partnerships in action and disruptive, box-destroying innovation.

Key Learning

1. Company buyers look for:
   (a) Revenue growth
   (b) Profit growth
   (c) Cash flow
   (d) Innovation
   (e) Management teams
2. Keys to increasing value:
   (a) Speed
   (b) Profitability
   (c) Cash flow
   (d) Capacity
   (e) Agility
3. Innovations and disruptive thinking drive dramatic improvement.

CHAPTER 6

The Dimensions of Executive Thought

Many executives, particularly of small and middle market companies, spend an inordinate amount of time attending to the details of the business rather than focusing on strategy and results. Top executives should be thinking about the direction and strategy of the company, and how they will translate that into action. Jack Welch, the former CEO of General Electric, once said that the two key roles of a CEO are to develop a company vision and to find the right people to implement it. This chapter will explore the four Dimensions of Executive Thought™ and how they drive results.

Financial

Financial returns are the first dimension. Many companies try to implement new approaches such as Lean, Re-engineering, or Six Sigma in an effort to reduce costs without asking the key question, "Are we getting a return on our investment?" In some cases, these efforts yield incremental improvements of 2 to 3 percent per year, but often they deliver no lasting improvement at all.

I frequently get calls from frustrated middle market company CEOs who say, "We've been doing Lean for three years now and we aren't making any more money. Should we be making more?" Management should anticipate an ROI from their efforts and expect the improvement to be sustained over time. In addition, they might also expect incremental improvements in the 10 to 20 percent range and higher.

At Alaska Communications, changing the way the company managed suppliers to an approach based on strong partnerships and auto-replenishment systems led to over $20 million in savings and productivity improvement, as well as an inventory reduction of over 200 percent. One high-ROI action was having a supplier deliver all construction materials (even materials they did not sell) to the site in a container, complete and ready to use, which eliminated downtime for construction teams in the field. Another way they boosted ROI was by improving technician productivity, allowing each of over 120 field service personnel to accomplish one to two additional jobs per day. The financial return from the improvement efforts was off the chart! Not only did productivity improve, but revenue increased, inventory decreased (releasing cash), and warehouse costs plummeted.

The process to accomplish that was both simple and innovative. Prior to the improvement effort, technicians began each day by taking inventory of their service vehicle, turning in their list at the parts counter, and then having coffee and socializing until their order was ready, which took 45 minutes or more. To eliminate this downtime, the company developed standard tool kits for the service vehicles that included two boxes for parts, as shown in Figure 6.1. The technicians would simply take their boxes to the parts counter and exchange them for new, fully stocked boxes. The company even considered having the parts suppliers provide

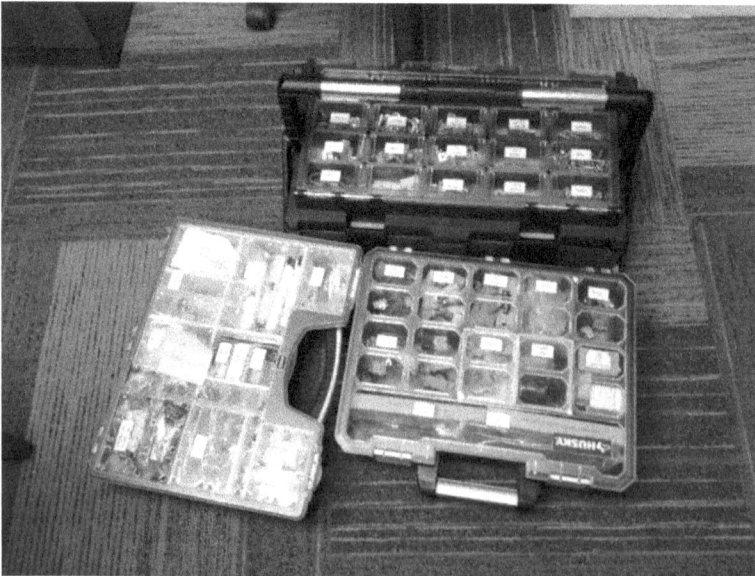

Figure 6.1 A fully stocked parts box

fully stocked kits and take the used ones to their warehouse at the end of each day for replenishment.

In addition to cutting the time it took to replenish the service vehicles to less than five minutes (and that was mostly for coffee), the number of stock keeping units was reduced by eliminating redundant parts, and inventory levels were reduced as well. The financial impact was astounding.

The impetus for financial performance improvement can come from markets, regulators, competitive changes, and technological changes. To help set financial expectations for improvement efforts, executives can ask:

- Are the financial returns about to change due to market conditions (for instance, are there new competitors coming into the market)? Are existing competitors engaged in productivity improvement? Are disruptive technologies coming into play?
- Is the regulatory environment about to impact your financial returns?
- Is the company achieving dramatic growth? Can your supply chains keep up, and do you have the necessary capacity and capital to support the growth?
- Is your banker satisfied with your financial results?
- Are other stakeholders happy?

Lean and many other process improvement methods are becoming the ante to play, rather than a competitive advantage. In the 1990s, total quality management (TQM) was a leading edge way to gain advantage over competitors, but when many companies jumped on the bandwagon TQM became passé. Today, Lean has become the process improvement approach that companies turn to, more out of fear of falling behind the pack than a desire to make radical profitability improvements.

That doesn't mean your company should not be using Lean to improve speed, profitability, cash flow, and capacity, but your competitors are using Lean, too. Because everyone is doing it, implementing Lean and continuous improvement does not automatically grant you a competitive advantage, rather companies like ACS that implement innovative ideas are the ones that will dramatically improve their financial outcomes.

Someone in the organization needs to be watching the horizon to spot the next generation of tools and methods to gain competitive advantage, even if it is fleeting. Companies like Zara and Amazon (and in earlier days, Toyota) are innovating their own processes to gain advantage in the market. Amazon developed innovative new ways to speed products to the consumers, while Zara developed a supply chain that could move high fashion women's wear from the designer to the store in as little as two weeks.

Many disruptive ideas come from the management level just below the top, and I refer to these people as the innovators in organizations because they often sponsor new, inventive ideas ranging from partnerships to speedy delivery, to extraordinary customer service (like Zappos). They are often the people that drive change and keep it on track, bridging the gap between executive visionaries and the people on the front lines. Without a continuous flow of innovative ideas, a company is like a stalled engine and nothing gets accomplished.

A prospect once said to me, "We've been growing almost 50 percent per year, but our profits have lagged. We work hard to grow our company, so shouldn't we be getting a return on our effort?" ROE—return on effort—is an excellent metric.

When looking at financial returns it's important to acknowledge that profit is not the only financial measure; cash flow is just as important, if not more so. Over the years, I have seen many companies that appeared to be profitable sink into the cash flow morass by holding too much inventory or by overinvesting in capital equipment, hoping for improved costs or production growth.

In Chapter 1 I introduced the concept of the cash-to-cash cycle as a key indicator of cash flow for the company:

Cash-to-cash cycle = A/R days + inventory days – A/P days.

There are some interesting behaviors in this model. For instance, in many companies the industry terms for both accounts payable and accounts receivable are about 35 days, so those two elements tend to offset each other.

That leaves inventory. Many small and mid-market manufacturers and distributors think that four turns is pretty good. In that case, about 90 days of cash is tied up in inventory. When I start working with some companies, I see turns as low as two (180 days) and one company had only one turn per year. Many companies show a cash-to-cash cycle of from 90 to 150 days. My best clients usually have a cycle of less than 50 days, and the world-class performers are under 20, while a few actually have a negative cash-to-cash cycle, meaning that they effectively get their cash before they spend it.

Who in the organization drives the cash-to-cash cycle? Most company managers assume the CFO is managing cash, so they don't think much about it. But in reality, how sales does its deals, how purchasing buys, how supply chain designs the distribution/warehouse network, how engineering designs products, and how marketing and product management bring new products to market and retire old ones all play major roles in the cash-to-cash cycle.

For example, if purchasing makes large volume buys in an effort to get deeper discounts, or if it buys truck-load quantities in an effort to reduce freight, that can have a negative impact on inventory turns, which increases cash consumption. If product management focuses on new products and not on old or obsolete products, the warehouses can accumulate obsolete inventory, which also consumes cash.

A 2017 article in *The Wall Street Journal*[1] revealed that Tesla was running low on cash as it ramped up production on a new model. Not only are there capital costs related to production, but also ramp-up of materials and parts enlarges inventory, especially for the period preceding production. Tesla had to look at debt or equity financing for the start-up cash management.

To manage cash flow effectively, companies must do more than just improve efficiency and save a few days of cash flow; they need disruptive thinking and innovation to really move the needle. Techniques such as supplier partnerships, auto-replenishment systems, effective terms with

---

[1] Wirz, M., and J.D. Stoll. August 7, 2017. "Tesla to Sell $1.5 Billion in Debt to Fuel Aggressive Expansion." *The Wall Street Journal* (accessed October 12, 2017).

suppliers and customers, product design for supply chain management (DFSCM), and just-in-time inventory and production can greatly reduce the need for cash and can be woven into the operations strategy.

Non-financial Returns

Non-financial returns are the company's growth drivers, but they may not be immediately measureable in dollars. They include consideration of local and global markets as well as product and service diversification. What's in your current portfolio of offerings to your customers, and do those offerings provide remarkable value? Are your supply chains set up to ensure timely and economical delivery of your products or services?

Many companies experience disruptive shifts in their markets that leave them behind. Think of cameras and music: Kodak and CDs were the immovable objects of the 1990s and now you rarely hear of either one.

When I was VP, operations at Supra, we implemented product refurbishment to increase revenue. We sold lockboxes to real estate agents that were often attached to hose bibs on the side of the house. Over time, they gathered mold, dirt, and began to look weathered. Agents liked nice-looking lockboxes; so for a small fee, we would replace the plastic cover, the shackle, and the key container so the box looked like new. We even offered custom colors to match their brokerage's color scheme.

The process required a whole new area in production to cut the old cover off and replace the three components, so we set up a complete reverse logistics process with a focus on quick turnaround time to get the boxes back into the field as quickly as possible.

While the program created a nice addition to our revenue, refurbishing the boxes allowed the agents to keep their investment working longer and improved the image of quality they liked to project. The reverse logistics process helped us extend our capabilities, which we used in other markets as well.

At another stage in Supra's diversification, we decided to open markets in China for our access control devices. We offered the ability to know when people entered a location by tracking where and when electronic keys were used. The most common application was access to remote cell

Figure 6.2 Tracking electronic key use on postboxes in China

tower sites for maintenance and other purposes. The unique application the Chinese wanted was for their postal delivery boxes, to prove that they could pick up and deliver mail on time. Figure 6.2 shows our device (the little rectangle on the lower door of the mailbox).

Resources

Companies need the right people in the right positions to implement strategy. The best strategy unimplemented is worthless; it's the proverbial notebook on the shelf that does nothing to accelerate profit and growth. Do you have the right people in the right positions? Should they be full-time, part-time, or temporary employees, and what skills should they have?

In many companies, overtime and temps are the only true variable costs in labor. In the short run as revenues go up and down, you cannot effectively release employees when you don't need them and then bring them back later. They will usually go find a more stable job and you lose the skills and experience they have, so in the short run labor is a fixed cost.

To transform some of your labor into variable cost, you can use both overtime and temps to supplement regular labor to handle peaks and valleys in shipments and service. Overtime can be used in a burst mode for short periods of time, but companies need to be careful not to burn people out. To maintain solid employee partnerships, it is important to coordinate overtime to help meet your needs while balancing the employees' work/life. Companies often ask for volunteers to work overtime to help meet that objective.

Using temps can also be effective. Many companies are hesitant to use temps because they see productivity and quality suffer when large numbers of temps are part of the labor force, but I have seen up to 35 percent and more of the workforce as temps used very effectively. There are a few vital elements that make that work.

1. Partner with one or two temp agencies to provide what you need. The agency can:
   a. Prescreen people for specific skills required for the job.
   b. Conduct basic training before they arrive in skills such as basic Lean concepts, and basic quality and inspection processes.
   c. Request that temps you have used before be selected first.
2. Partner with your employees for effective temp use.
   a. Develop a mentor program so experienced employees work alongside the temps to help them be successful.
   b. Give your employees the right to fire temps or request they be replaced.
3. Partner with the temps.
   a. Include them as part of the teams on the floor, including attending informational meetings and training.
   b. Treat them like employees.

As partnerships grow, you can expect exponential improvements in materials costs, inventory turns, customer order fulfillment levels, and the ability to get new products to market effectively. Supplier partners can help organize your supply chain for profit and growth, while internal partnerships can help prevent functional silos and encourage interdepartmental cooperation and strong teams.

Partnerships benefit both parties, creating win/win relationships that achieve success beyond what the parties could have done alone. True partnerships offer many advantages:

- World-class pricing and competitiveness
- Greater profitability for both parties
- More flexibility and agility
- Enhanced quality
- Increased return on assets
- A feeling of teamwork and success
- Pride in results

The best partnerships use a small number of very close relationships, like, for example, using a small number of suppliers (perhaps only two) to provide a particular commodity. It could be having a one-on-one relationship between production and sales for planning purposes. Successful partnerships are based on liaison and trust and are built through consistent, direct, mutually beneficial connections.

Technology

Technology is moving more rapidly every day, and companies need expertise (either within their ranks or outside the organization) to determine whether technology is hype or high-ROI for their business's specific goals. The Internet of Things, Big Data, SaaS, mobile devices, and social networks dramatically impact corporate relationships with customers, suppliers, and even employees. Can you use technology to increase speed throughout your value chain? Should your company be more or less dependent on technology, and if you do choose to implement new technology, can it be done rapidly and without disruption?

Many companies assume that automation is the solution to high labor costs, but automating processes render them more difficult to change and improve. Before implementing new technology, executives should examine the process and determine if it can be simplified or even eliminated altogether, thereby avoiding the time and expense of automating a process that wasn't necessary in the first place.

While automation is rarely more flexible than human interaction, repetitive and high-precision tasks can often benefit from automation. Industrial robots are certainly one example of that. A past client, a custom metal fabricator, found that the welding cell was the bottleneck in the plant and, in an effort to reduce lead and cycle times and improve quality, they began using robotic welders for certain repetitive tasks. The welding robots were very effective for those tasks and allowed one person to run three production areas.

I advise caution when implementing automation for two reasons:

1. Automation can be difficult to change, and creates monuments that are inflexible. Nothing is more adaptable than a human being.
2. A strong focus on automation often masks the real delay in the system.

For example, a different client also believed their welding cell was the bottleneck. However, further investigation showed that in fact, the sales order entry process and work order development were delaying orders by as much as two weeks. By simply changing work assignments for a couple of people in the office, order processing time was cut from two weeks to less than a day. Not only did that significantly change customer order lead times, which improved competitiveness, it also shifted the bottleneck on the floor to an area that had previously received little attention.

Key Learning

There are four Dimensions of Executive Thought™:

1. Financial
2. Non-financial
3. Resources
4. Technology

Executives need to consider all four dimensions to accelerate profit and growth. Developing the vision and getting the right people in the right positions are the CEO's two essential roles. Looking at these four dimensions and keeping an eye on the big picture are vital to rapidly moving the company to greater results.

CHAPTER 7

You Aren't in This Alone

The CEO or owner of the company cannot drive value by him or herself. Developing the business vision and strategy and aligning it with the operations strategy requires the participation of the company's key executives, and the executives and managers involved in operations should participate in developing the operations strategy. This not only allows for a more holistic view, but also keeps the key players invested in the process. This chapter explores how constructing great teams leads to successful strategy development and drives exponential results.

Many middle market companies limit their strategy development process to an annual off-site retreat. The morning of the first day is usually spent going over the results from the current or past year, and the afternoon is spent on the golf course. The second day is devoted to a strengths, weaknesses, opportunities, and threats (SWOT) analysis, with the last hour or two spent thinking about "strategic initiatives" for the coming year, usually related to the weaknesses identified in the SWOT analysis or to improving profitability. The main preparation for the retreat is on the part of the CFO, who brings updated financials and perhaps a first draft of the budget for the coming year.

Often in small and medium-sized companies (SMEs), the CEO or owner will try to develop the overall business strategy on their own, relying on their executive team to develop the implementation plan, often in a vacuum. The executive team should develop the "what" and "why" of strategy, while the various departments should then develop the "how." For example, in a company with a full complement of C-level executives and vice presidents, the top executives should develop the road map for reaching the vision. I believe they should also have input to the vision, though that often comes from the board or owner. Once the roadmap is identified, the various teams should then develop their departmental strategies in support of the overall strategy.

The company's close outside advisers provide another vital resource for executives. I believe that every company needs a council of advisers made up of their banker, outside CPA, attorney, and any consultants who help with executive coaching, strategy development, and major improvement projects. These advisers provide an outside perspective on the company's performance and can offer input on the improvement initiatives that would best serve the company in the near term. They also contribute economic, market, and regulatory insight to the strategy development process.

Many SME companies have a long-standing relationship with an individual CPA or a small CPA firm that focuses primarily on taxes or a review for the bank, but many CPA firms now provide a broader array of services that can contribute to growth and improve strategy. The same goes for an active commercial banker, who can often provide services related to international transactions (both incoming and outgoing), debt financing, capital budgeting and financing, wealth management, and other areas that help build the foundation for strategic initiatives. Including the commercial banker in the strategy development process, at least for input and discussing the company's options, can be very beneficial.

In preparation for writing this book, I interviewed the top executives of six middle market companies, ranging in size from $30 million to over $600 million in revenue, all of them successful, growing companies. Interestingly, the number of participants in their planning processes ranged from one, with input from division presidents, to 50 or 60. Despite this variation, the companies that are growing with great purpose and vision follow similar practices in involving people in the planning process.

The six companies spanned a number of industries including:

- Ship repair
- Packing equipment for the beverage industry
- Recreational equipment manufacturing and distribution
- Exercise equipment built offshore and distributed via multiple channels
- A producer and installer of kitchen cabinets
- A mini-conglomerate comprised of multiple businesses, all distributed through retail

In four of the six, the CEO led the planning process, and the CFO or COO took the reins at the remaining two companies. Coincidentally, those two had a much less rigorous process than the four that were led from the top.

The most successful companies followed a very deliberate planning process that often lasted three months or more. In some cases, the executive team developed the company vision and strategy, and then the upper management levels (second layer) tested it for feasibility. There was typically no off-site retreat because the planning process was engrained in the executive team's monthly activities.

The Strategy Team

The planning team at the companies I examined was typically made up of the top-level executives of each operating department along with the CEO or owner. Again, that team developed the strategic framework and the result was tested for feasibility by the next level down in the organization, which provided feedback. Three of the companies then presented the final draft to their board for their input. In only one case did the strategy start at the board level, and that was a family-owned business where family members sat on the board.

Three of the companies worked on planning every month, and in one case every week. One CEO said that he spent 75 to 80 percent of his time "looking at the future." In the companies where the CEO did not lead the process, the other executives often felt the process could be stronger.

The executive teams were most often comprised of:

- CEO
- COO/VP, operations
- CFO/director of finance
- VPs of sales, administration, systems, service/field operations, product development/engineering
- Business unit managers

The total number of people involved at the business strategy development level was typically from 6 to 8, although one company had as many as 50 people involved in some point in the process.

It can be difficult to determine how many people should be involved in the planning process. The easy answer is, "Everyone necessary, but no more." Too many cooks can spoil the process. Companies might try to involve a lot of people, but some will end up bored because there are so many people that they don't get to really participate. Others will see the process as an interruption of their normal duties. In the spirit of simplification, pick only the key managers and executives that can really be additive to the process, and determine how to communicate the results as part of the plan. Remember that people can be pulled into the process as needed to provide information and ideas without necessarily being involved in the entire process.

In three of the companies, once they had developed their business strategy, each operating department went through a planning process to set strategy and implementation in their specific area. One company's VP, operations, had a very formal planning process for operations that included:

- VP, operations
- Director of supply chain
- Quality
- Sourcing
- Logistics
- Distribution
- Planning and inventory

That company also met with their suppliers to assess risk.

One company, once they had developed their overall strategy, sent it to the next level in the organization to develop implementation plans. They did this because the company is very diverse in its products and services, and the various parts of the company have widely varying business models and different standards for success. The company philosophy is to have the implementers do the detailed planning and define resource requirements.

The most successful companies involved the following people and/or groups in strategy development:

Company level:

- CEO/owner (leader of strategy development)
- All "C" level or VP-level people, typically CFO, COO/VP (operations), VP (engineering/product development), VP (sales), VP (field service), VP (admin/systems), and business unit leaders
- Corporate board of directors (if there is one)

Department level:

- VP, operations
- Quality
- Supply chain/procurement
- Distribution/logistics
- Plant management (if there is one)

Most of the companies specifically mentioned an operations strategy, but did not mention other department plans tied to the company strategy. Often the operations strategy included detailed resource needs along with the supply chain strategy that would be used for product manufacturing/acquisition, as well as the distribution model they would use for order fulfillment. A couple of companies considered the distribution model to be a key competitive advantage, which is why they developed a specific strategy for it.

Obviously the operations strategy is developed after the business strategy, but the COO/VP (operations') direct involvement in creating the business strategy is important to provide input related to core operations capabilities that might provide competitive advantage.

Partnerships

In my book, *1 + 1 = 100: Achieving Breakthrough Results Through Partnerships*, I guided readers through developing, implementing, and maintaining close relationships within the company (employees, engineering, product development, sales and marketing, operations, and supply chain) as well as outside the company (suppliers, customers, and the community). I believe that partnerships yield better products, better relationships with suppliers, and better outcomes for customers and stakeholders.

Partnerships provide a win/win foundation that gives both parties the opportunity to achieve success beyond what they could have accomplished alone. True partnerships offer many advantages:

- World-class pricing and competitiveness
- Greater profitability
- More flexibility and agility
- Enhanced quality
- Increased return on assets
- Stronger teamwork
- Pride in results

Including your partners in the strategy development process can significantly improve growth and profitability. A survey of 435 top automotive suppliers found that the Big Three (Ford, General Motors, and Fiat Chrysler) had weak supplier relationships costing them over $2 billion in sales in 2014.[1]

Developing and using partnerships in the supply chain is an example of a strategic initiative that would be developed by the operations team, but should be included as a business strategy because of the potential impacts on speed to market, technical capabilities, and other areas. Implementing partnerships is more than just a tactic; it can change the business model in significant ways.

Supplier partnerships go deeper than collaboration, which is simply working with another company toward a joint outcome. Partnerships involve a closer relationship that pulls the partners together, to their mutual benefit. Qualifying and maintaining those relationships,

---

[1] Putre, L. 2015 "Weak Supplier Relations Costing Big 3 Automakers, Nissan Billions: Survey." *IndustryWeek.com*, May 17. http://industryweek.com/supplier-relationships/weak-supplier-relations-costing-big-3-automakers-nissan-billions-survey (accessed October 15, 2017).

understanding a partner's capabilities, and maximizing results require commitment and investment. The decisions and resources required to implement and use partnerships belong at the strategic level, and partnership initiatives should be included in both the business and operations strategy frameworks. I have seen companies reduce inventory by over 200 percent, substantially increase cash flow, and cut materials costs by 10 to 20 percent in 12 to 18 months, all by implementing partnerships.

Other partnership-related issues such as using temporary workers, sheltered workshops, third-party logistics distribution, and quick product development can all impact the overall business strategy. Perhaps one of the best examples is Zara, the Spanish clothing company. Their business and operations strategy is based on speed. They can move women's fashions from design to store in about two weeks—much faster than the competition—which generates customer demand and revenue levels unmatched in the industry. That is not a tactical approach, but rather a strategy that permeates the entire organization. Jobs are kept local, which builds a partnership with the community.

Process Owners

Every process within a company needs an owner: *one* person accountable for the process. While there can be several people responsible for various elements or steps, there needs to be only one owner. Through working with many clients over the years, I've found that, when several people own a process, nobody owns it.

I like to use the RACI process to help define ownership. RACI is a matrix that assigns participants to a process's main tasks. There are four categories of assignment:

1. Responsibility
2. Accountability
3. Consult
4. Inform

This form, shown in Figure 7.1, is especially useful in clarifying roles and responsibilities in cross-functional and cross-departmental projects and processes. When I introduce this concept to my clients, people understand it quickly, and, more importantly, they seem to appreciate the clarification it provides.

The roles are:

- Responsible—those who are assigned work or outcomes from the process or task
- Accountable—the one who makes the final decision, the approver
- Consulted—those whose input is sought before the task or process is undertaken
- Informed—those who are informed of what has been done.

The form itself appears as follows:

Process—Purchasing and inventory

	Materials	Production	Distribution	Quality	Mfg.Eng.	Sales	Finance
Ordering	R	A	C	I			
Logistics							
Inventory							
Suppliers							
Controls							
Policies							

R = Responsible   A = Accountable C = Consulted I = Informed

Figure 7.1 RACI process-owner form

A culture of accountability is important for strategy implementation, and process ownership is part of that. As an example, let's look at a retail company I worked with whose sales had trended downward for 12 to 18 months. There could have been several reasons for it, but one thing that stood out was the empty shelves in the stores. Every time I visited one of their stores, the same shelves were empty. If products weren't readily available, some customers would ask for them, but many would simply go down the street to a competitor to find what they needed, and potential sales were being lost.

First, I asked who owned stock replenishment. The answer certainly shed some light on the problem: no one. People on the sales floor replenished stock as time allowed but, as busy as they were, time allowed for very little, and employees typically stocked shelves when it was convenient, usually at the end of the shift, or in response to a special request. Lack of accountability was costing the company its reputation as well as revenue.

Operations strategy should include RACI to define roles and responsibilities for each major process addressed in the strategy. Even the strategy development process itself can use RACI to define strategy development roles. The CEO should own company strategy, being the A for company strategy. The COO/VP (operations) should own operations strategy, thus being an R for company strategy and an A for operations strategy. These top executives, and only they, can be held accountable for strategy development and implementation. Others who participate would clearly have responsibilities, but one owner. Others in the organization that were not directly involved in the planning process might play roles in the C and I categories.

Key Learning

- The CEO or company should lead business strategy development.
- Key executives should be involved in the process.
- Each key business area (e.g., operations, sales, or product development) should then develop their own strategy to support the overall business strategy and include the key managers/directors in their area.
- Too many cooks spoil the soup. Be careful not to involve too many people in an effort to build consensus.
- Consult outside partners and advisers for input and perspective on important issues.
- Get process owners involved in operating department-level planning. Each process should have one, and only one, owner.

CHAPTER 8

Focus on Results

Is your company working the way it was designed to in the business strategy? Does that strategy energize your stakeholders? This chapter lays out ways to define and measure progress, build accountability, and avoid the trap of failure work that many executives fall into.

Many companies question whether they are doing the right things, doing things right, and getting the results they should be getting. Executives often rely on statistics collected by industry associations, which usually show industry averages, but why aim for average results? Falling in the top 25 percent of industry achievement would be good, and reaching the top 10 percent would be great.

Is It Good?

There are also nonnumerical means of gauging results. In the *Book of Genesis*, God looked at His creation and said, "It is good," meaning that it was working the way He designed it. In addition, theologians suggest it also means that God is enjoying His creation. As a business owner or executive, can you say the same about your business? What would make you enjoy your creation?

There are two key aspects of being able to say, "It is good," about your business. The first is design, which is evident in the business model. The business model outlines how the business will make money, who the customers are, what products or services the company will offer, any additional revenue sources, and the details of financing the business. The design includes the vision, which states what you want your business to look like in the future. A clear vision illuminates the organization's goals and helps your employees understand their role in achieving them.

Many small and mid-market companies don't take the time to develop a vision or even to plan beyond the next 12 months. For example, the

CEO of a lower mid-market company wondered why his employees weren't achieving what he wanted; and when I asked about the vision, a quizzical look came over his face and he said he didn't have one, and he just wanted people to take care of customers and ship on time. He had provided no context, no targets, and no way for the employees to know if they were accomplishing anything. I guess he should have just given them all a participation trophy and hoped for the best.

A strong design includes an operations strategy that aligns with the business vision and overall strategy. Not only does this create the lift your business needs to reach new heights, but a strong design can yield speed, service, quality, and cost improvements, generating a significant competitive advantage.

The second aspect of being able to say "It is good" is knowing on a day-to-day, week-to-week, or month-to-month basis that the design of your business is working the way you intended. The first and most obvious metric is that you are getting the desired results. Many executives focus on activities such as sales, Lean, team building, and new product introduction, but executives need to focus on results, not activities, which are the realm of the management team. Focusing on results helps drive performance and takes you to your vision.

The business design's success impacts external stakeholders as well, including owners, suppliers, customers, your bank, and the community. A rising tide raises all ships. By focusing on the benefits to all partners, your business can maximize results to a level beyond belief.

Measuring Results

Measures provide the feedback that you and your team need to know whether the organization is on track. Of the six companies I interviewed for this book, only three had well-defined key performance measures (KPMs) tied to both the business strategy and operations strategy. The other three relied on financial measures and more general indicators, such as whether plans were in place. One used the "gut feel" of how the business was doing as a measure.

The three companies that had more definitive measures typically had four primary measures and several secondary measures, which I equate to the dashboard of a small aircraft that has a big dial (typically the artificial horizon), surrounded by four midsized dials (altimeter, compass, airspeed, and rate of climb), and a number of smaller indicators.

What measures are used will tend to vary by company type, but the four key measures are usually revenue growth, profit growth, cash flow, and quality. Some companies might use a few specifically related to their industries such as capitation rate for insurance companies, units shipped for remanufacturers, number of projects for landscaping, and so on. Tying the measures to the key priorities developed in the planning process will help identify what they should be. Be careful not to create too many top-level measures as that can get confusing as to where the priorities need to be.

Some of the specific measures that companies employed included:

- Revenue—daily, weekly, monthly, often broken down by market segment
- Bookings—year-over-year
- Units sold
- Quality
- Labor—plan to actual
- Capacity and equipment loading
- Total productive maintenance
- Rework
- Head count
- Material costs as a percent of revenue
- Number of bids issued/number of wins
- Overtime
- Safety
- New orders from new customers
- Balance sheet strength

In each case, the companies selected measures that tied directly to their strategies and plans, choosing three to five key measures for the business strategy and three to five for the operations strategy. Most reviewed them monthly at executive meetings and quarterly with the board, if they had one. Some companies reviewed them weekly at management team meetings, with particular attention to gaps in performance and indications of possible problems. Those with strong KPMs had highly engaged management teams and employees.

One of the most useful reports is a simple daily flash report. Usually an Excel spreadsheet, this report lists the items that are key to your success, such as daily shipments (revenue), inventory and other working capital components, shipped-on-time, and near-term priorities such as overtime. The report's contents should reflect the company's priorities and specific gap issues that need immediate attention, such as excess overtime. It is also useful in helping plan activities, such as how many shipments are needed per day to meet the monthly goal. The daily flash report can yield significant additional profit because it illuminates issues as they occur, rather than waiting for the monthly financial reports.

One of the key benefits of KPMs is that they help you and your team focus on results rather than activities, and prevent you from falling into the "busy trap." Unfortunately, an element of human behavior is that, when we don't know what to do, we tend to run in circles, staying busy but accomplishing very little. Good leaders armed with solid KPMs get everyone to settle down, focus on priorities, and get results.

Measuring results helps reinforce priorities and keeps the team focused on what is important. Mid-level managers in particular need to avoid the busy trap of day-to-day urgencies (the "putting out fires" phenomenon), and instead keep driving toward their goals.

Smart companies design their metrics to drive innovation as much as (or more than) efficiency. Often companies set targets for improvement that are too low and don't drive revolutionary change. Don't just ask for 2 to 3 percent improvement; ask for 10 or 20 percent. The only way to achieve that is to think outside the box and innovate.

Visualizing

Your vision—the future state you are trying to achieve—sets the agenda for the near term. Typically, the time frame for a vision should be 18 to 36 months, an actionable time frame that keeps things relevant while being long enough to allow time to incorporate feedback.

Ownership

Communication
and culture

Leader's vision

Action pyramid

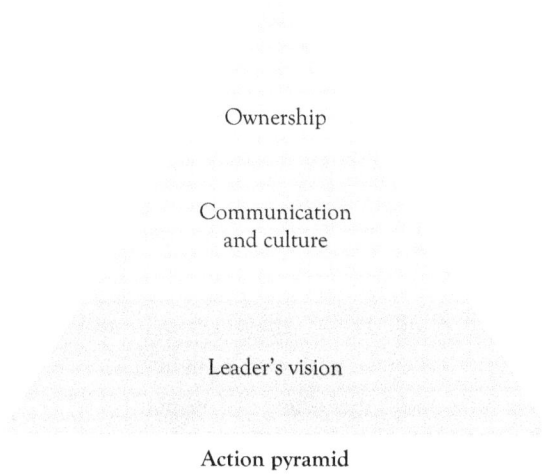

Figure 8.1 The leader's vision sets the foundation for action

Clarifying the results you want to achieve helps your team understand where they are going and why. A strong vision focuses on value for your customers, stakeholders, and employees. Focusing on the big picture lets you step away from the day-to-day tactical issues that so often capture too much management and executive attention. The vision allows executives to make well-considered decisions and measure progress.

As shown in Figure 8.1, the leader's vision, combined with strong internal communication and culture, sets the foundation for action, which leads to ownership of results.

Strategic Myopia

Myopia is typically referred to as nearsightedness, a condition where close objects appear clearly, but objects in the distance look blurry. Strategic myopia occurs when executives only see or consider the issues that are right in front of them. That could be due to priority, familiarity, or, more importantly, having blinders on. Many times, executives focus singularly on shipping products or delivering services to the customers. While that is obviously important, the priorities set in the strategy may be broader. Sometimes you have to get out of the business to work on the business, and day-to-day priorities can be an impediment to that.

Lorraine Moore, a strategy and leadership consultant with Accelerate Success Group, suggests that strategic myopia is the inability to recognize potential obstacles and opportunities in the long term, including potential disruptors to the business or new markets. She suggests that a balanced view of near-term and longer-term issues is important in strategy development.

When executives focus on activities rather than results, they exacerbate their myopia because, by their very nature, activities tend to be narrow in scope. Executives should be standing on the proverbial mountaintop surveying the entire business battlefield to see how strategies should change to support the vision and respond to changing strategic issues. Their executive and management teams must respond to events on the battlefield.

During World War II, one reason the German Blitzkrieg was so successful was that German generals set a very clear strategy and vision for what they wanted to achieve. Then they made their field and individual tank commanders responsible for the day-to-day decisions they encountered. The result was a very fast advance that kept the British off-balance and resulted in the evacuations recently depicted in the movie "Dunkirk."

Several of the executives I interviewed said that their teams continuously reviewed their strategy to identify shortcomings and gaps in performance. They could adjust as needed to provide the greatest return and flexibility in how they moved toward their vision. In several cases, teams reviewed their strategies quarterly, and a few did it semiannually. The lowest- performing companies reviewed strategy only at their annual strategy sessions.

The keys to avoiding myopia are:

1. Having a clear vision, typically 18 to 36 months
2. Using key measures to provide hard data on performance
3. Continuously measuring performance against goals to identify gaps
4. Taking action with accountability

Avoiding Failure Work

I often refer to failure work as the black hole of profit. A black hole is a place in space where gravity's force is so strong that even light can't get out. Because there is no light, we can't see black holes, yet we know they exist. Failure work in business—the process of correcting things that are wrong, taking contingent action, or putting out fires—is much the same: it exists, it consumes resources, and it often goes unnoticed.

Failure work includes:

- Rework
- Mis-shipments
- Bad quality
- Scrap
- Obsolete inventory
- Inspection
- Errors

Fundamentally, failure work encompasses any activity that requires time and resources to be spent correcting mistakes.

Unfortunately failure work costs even more than the core cost of repeating the work, since materials often need to be expedited, labor is supplemented with overtime, or an extra shift has to be added to catch up. This can cost one and one half times more than it would have to do it right the first time.

The maxim "Do It Right the First Time" was commonplace in the early days of total quality management and Six Sigma, but seems to have diminished with the advent of Kaisen, Lean, and continuous improvement. While companies continue to focus on eliminating waste, many waste-reduction activities are driven by problem solving and corrective action, rather than by designing processes to be failure-proof (Poke-Yoke is the Japanese term).

Problem solving is a corrective action. The problem has already occurred, and now extra resources are needed to fix it. My mentor Alan Weiss suggests that problem solving occurs when there is a deviation from the norm, and it simply brings you back to where you were.

To prevent failure work, companies need to shift from a policy of corrective action to preventative action by designing processes so they can be done right the first time and minimize the need for failure work. I use the term operations discipline to describe this emphasis on doing it right the first time.

Strong operations discipline dramatically reduces failure work, thereby improving quality, cost, delivery, and customer satisfaction. While customers appreciate your ability to solve their problems, they prefer to not have problems in the first place. The same is true for the internal chain of customers, like the link between customer service and order picking and shipping, engineering and production, warehouse and shipping, and shipping and accounting. We'll look at operations discipline in more detail in Chapter 9.

There are three ways to failure proof your processes. First, you need to have a process: a defined way of doing things that's been tested to avoid mistakes. This creates a preventative action, known as standard work in Lean companies. Well-designed processes help prevent failure work.

Next, you need a culture of accountability that supports doing things right the first time, including clear instruction and training. Outcomes need to be measured to let people know how they are doing and those measures should focus on results, not activity.

Third, rules and constructs need to be in place to ensure that processes are accomplished on time. For example, in many warehouses, teams allow received items to sit on the loading dock or in a receiving location for several days before checking them in and putting them away. Not only can that delay customer shipments but, since the inventory system can't "see" the items that are waiting on the dock, purchasing might order more, thinking they are almost out of materials, causing overstock and low inventory turns.

One practice many of my clients use is "A Day's Work in A Day," which applies not only to stocking materials, but also to any processing step such as order entry, invoicing, payroll processing, and returned goods processing. A day's work in a day means that you don't go home until the day's work is done, including data entry and paperwork, as shown in Figure 8.2. It is amazing how much more productive people can be with this rule in place.

Initiatives to eliminate failure work can be included in your operations plan, and doing it right the first time should be part of the operations vision. Eliminating the black hole of failure work will drive increased profit, cash flow, and capacity to support accelerated growth.

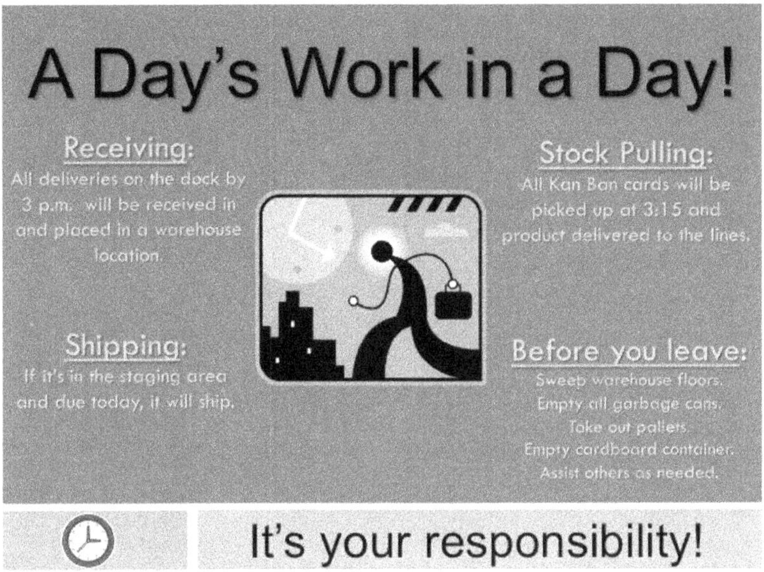

Figure 8.2 A day's work in a day

Key Learning

- Good results start with:
  - o Good design and a strong business model and vision
  - o Getting the results you expect
- Measures provide feedback and create a culture of account-ability.
- The vision defines the future state, sets the agenda, and helps people understand the "why" of what they are doing.
- Avoid strategic myopia by focusing on long-term goals and by not getting lost in the weeds of day-to-day activity.
- Failure work is the black hole of business, consuming resources and profitability.

CHAPTER 9

Creating an Action Imperative™

Change management can be one of the most frustrating activities that executives undertake. Many companies are trying to improve productivity, implement Lean thinking, innovate across the company, and generally improve performance, competitiveness, and overall company value, but at the same time middle-level managers are just trying to keep their heads above water, accomplishing their day-to-day tasks. This renders middle management unable to carry out change management initiatives, which slows down the change, or even completely cripples it.

An Action Imperative™ may be the missing link that empowers managers to follow through with change management initiatives, brings innovation efforts to fruition, and delivers sustainable results. An Action Imperative has three elements: change management, continuous improvement, and culture development. You'll need to develop a vision that motivates others, understand what real continuous improvement can do for the company, and know how to recruit or develop the right people and put them in the right positions in order to get results.

Operations Discipline

There is an old story that if you drop a frog into boiling water he will jump out, but if you put the frog into cold water and gradually turn up the heat he will cook. While somewhat gruesome, that is an apt description of what happens when organizations lack operations discipline. They slowly die of increased costs, increased inventory, employee morale problems, and weak customer service.

Operations discipline, which we touched on briefly in Chapter 8, is the willingness to create and adhere to processes and hold people accountable for performing them. In Lean speak, this includes standard work,

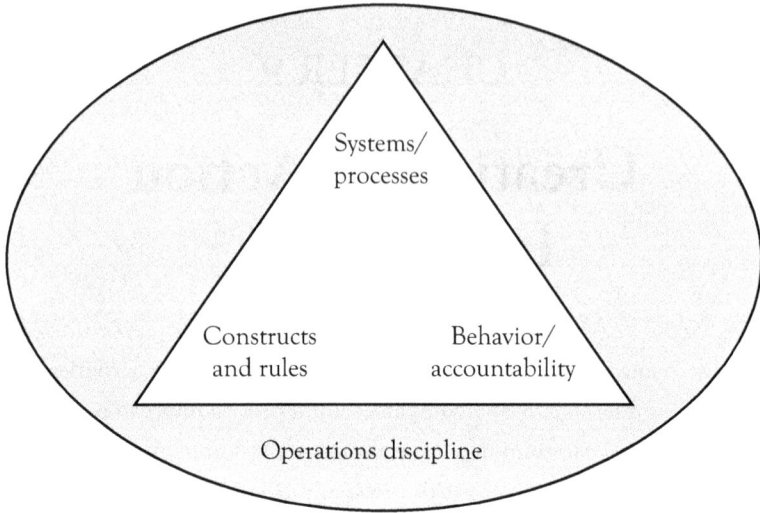

Figure 9.1 Operations discipline

whereby each process is clearly defined and performed the same way every time. This removes randomness from the process, improves quality, and provides consistent results, the core of standard work. It also creates a foundation for continuous improvement, since the target for improvement should be processes, not people.

Over the years I have encountered a number of companies whose culture does not hold people accountable for following the process, where even simple things like adhering to a standard part number structure are nonexistent or unenforced. The results are excess inventory, rising costs, high obsolescence, and other things that look like the frog slowly cooking. Operations discipline, shown in Figure 9.1, helps turn off the heat.

Systems and Processes

An operational environment is comprised of a series of processes that, taken together, create a system that delivers what the customer wants, when they want it at the lowest possible cost. Acknowledging those processes as building blocks allows companies to identify opportunities for continuous improvement.

Improvement can only occur in an environment where the processes are clearly defined and understood. Understanding the processes—knowing how they should be working and how they are currently working—reveals gaps where continuous improvement can be applied to achieve better results.

Constructs and Rules

Albert Einstein said, "You have to learn the rules of the game. And then you have to play better than anyone else." Constructs and rules are the guidelines to the processes and procedures in a system. Operations discipline cannot exist without constructs and rules. Here is an example of what can happen without appropriate constructs and rules.

A $100-million construction-related business had four people in their purchasing department and 82 actual buyers. It's generally alright that more than just the four purchasers were authorized to buy, but this is where constructs and rules are essential. With so many people in different departments and locations all buying without clear rules, things had become a mess. For example, many of the people doing the buying didn't know who the company's authorized suppliers were, which created an explosion of part numbers and suppliers, resulting in too much inventory and excessive obsolete inventory. In addition, any opportunity to take advantage of increased volume discounts disappeared.

Another issue at this company was temporary items. When the company got a new project, they often needed supplies that they didn't normally carry and for which there were no established part numbers or descriptions in the system. Without a standard way to look up new parts, buyers would inevitably create a new part number and a new description over and over for the same part, resulting in endless duplication and making it impossible to track parts accurately. There were about 17,000 active parts, but when we counted the actual number of parts in the part master file including all of the duplicates we found 164,000. The problem arose out of a genuine desire to do right by the customer, but without constructs and rules chaos reigned.

Behavior and Accountability

Have you ever attended (or sent a subordinate to attend) a professional development seminar, only to come back to work and never use the new skills or information? Have you embarked on a Lean journey only to discover a few years later that the changes didn't stick or didn't yield the desired results? Have you toured other companies to see how they do things, only to return to your company and never apply what you learned? Creating a Culture of Action™ requires behavior changes accompanied by accountability; in other words, you have to act and motivate others to act, and hold people, including yourself, accountable.

A single action is not enough to create a sustainable pattern of activity and, without repeated action over time, the change process will grind to a halt. The second law of thermodynamics, shown in Figure 9.2, says that any system that is not improving will sink into chaos.

Companies that can transform single actions into habits can sustain a change effort over the long term. Repeating the action and measuring results to instill accountability help turn actions into habits and habits into culture. A culture of action yields sustainable results.

One means of reinforcing the culture is through the evaluation process, which begins with the vision.

- Review and revise the vision for the company or department.
- Distill and record the basic values embodied in the vision.
- For each value define the specific behaviors that will make the vision a reality.
- Include those behaviors in hiring and evaluations.

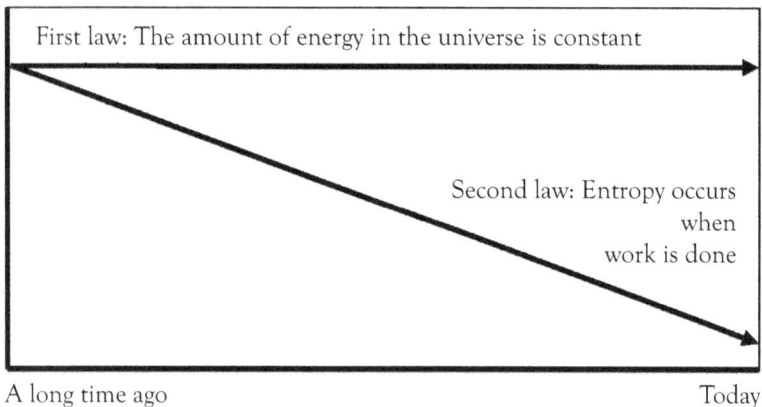

First law: The amount of energy in the universe is constant

Second law: Entropy occurs when work is done

A long time ago   Today

Figure 9.2 A system that is not improving will sink into chaos

When we implemented world-class manufacturing at Supra, one of the first things we did was to overhaul the entire employee evaluation process to include things like team participation, communication, and quality. Essentially, we built the things we wanted to improve into the evaluation process, and we paid people based on their results. That got commitment!

Achieving Breakthrough Results

"We're so good at being good that we forget to be great," I heard a CFO say during the opening remarks at a management retreat. As I thought about this, it occurred to me that many businesses have taken shelter under the awning of "good." To survive this economy, companies rely on cost reduction, cash conservation, labor efficiency, and stronger bank relationships to weather the storm. They focus every day on being good, but they forget that other companies are preparing for growth and striving to be great. Even world-class athletes are always striving to be better, to be great, because they know that, if they slack off, someone will sweep by them to win the gold.

What is great? Great is unwavering focus on the customer, which means delivering what the customer wants, when they want it. Great is providing quality, service, and everything else your customers crave, to build advantage that others cannot copy. The customer defines quality, and the most important measure is speed.

Good is using technology and cost reduction and, though these may drive some markets, they offer only a fleeting advantage. Anyone can implement Lean (although many that do fail to reap lasting benefits), and anyone can buy technology. Many companies have tried to cost-cut their way to success, but growth is the best way to survive in any economy.

One of my clients is making hay by providing reliable lead times and top quality. Even though customers could get lower prices from a competitor that has shifted production to Mexico and China, the competitor's unreliable deliveries erode their customers' overall profitability. My client has the opportunity to grow substantially by focusing on quality and shipped-on-time.

Great is constant innovation combined with effective change management. Innovation can mean creating new products, but it can also mean constantly pushing the limits of growth, service, quality, and cost. Process innovation is a function of change management and striving to improve in all aspects of business.

Great companies capitalize on their improvements, sometimes in ways that weren't obvious at first glance. For example, a client was looking into materials recycling as a process innovation. Not only would it cut their materials costs by as much as 10 percent, but it would position them as a green company helping its customers create a sustainable supply stream. In turn, their customers can pass on the added value to their customers.

Great is continuous improvement, but not the way we understand it today. Continuous improvement is a management approach of constant small upgrades that lead to competitive advantage by giving the customers what they want, when they want it, at the lowest possible cost.

Many companies see Lean or the Toyota Production System as a problem-solving technique that uses various tools to reduce costs and increase productivity, but reactive problem solving tends to create a stifling atmosphere of cost-consciousness.

Keeping employees engaged in the process rather than relying on "drive-by Kaisens" to improve is the most powerful way to increase competitiveness. Great is hard to copy. Great is relentless innovation with a focus on the customer that provides long-term competitive advantage.

Back in the days when Lean was known as world-class manufacturing, many companies had the goal of 5 percent productivity improvements year on year. They typically looked at operations as the source, gleaning improvements from labor and suppliers. When they started their transformation, they may have achieved 10 percent or even 15 percent improvements the first year, but they nearly always failed to sustain that level of improvement.

In an article in BusinessWeek,[1] Applied Materials CEO Michael Splinter shared how he intended to respond to the ups and downs of the industry as well as a 50 percent sales drop in 2000. He said, "We are managing our operations differently. We have record employee productivity."

---

[1] "Cleverly Chasing the Chip Boom." *BusinessWeek*, June 21, 2004.

At that time, they began achieving 10 to 15 percent improvement every year. To continue to achieve this level of improvement, companies need to apply innovative thinking to the entire business process, from order to delivery and from supplier to customer.

The way orders are presented to operations can have a major impact on operations productivity. Expediting, inserting other orders into the flow, and changing orders can erode speed and productivity. Some people think the eighth waste of Lean is interruptions, because any interruption hurts productivity. Some studies suggest that if an engineer is interrupted by a phone call or e-mail, it takes up to 20 minutes for them to get back into the groove of their work.

The key to process improvement is to manage the entire process as a single entity. Some companies carefully measure the time from receiving an order to the order's first production step, but for the customer that time is waste and non-value adding. By focusing on reducing the wasted time between receiving an order and getting it into production, companies can exponentially reduce lead times. One client, a service organization, cut their lead time from 40 days to just 14 hours.

Why Don't Things Get Done?

I hear this question from many frustrated CEOs, CFOs, COOs, and managers. People go into meetings to discuss important issues and problems, but when they leave the meeting nothing changes. Three things contribute to this frustrating situation:

1. Too many priorities
2. Lack of accountability
3. Lack of follow-up

Employees need to know which tasks are high priorities. People at all levels are being assigned more work as a result of cutbacks in response to economic downturns and efforts to increase business value in preparation for a transition, as well as "normal" improvement activities such as Lean or Six Sigma. New products, new projects, training, additional work due to someone leaving the company, and just plain growth, all cause employee workloads to swell.

A wise person once said, "It is better to move three things forward a mile than a thousand things forward an inch." To help people get things done, top management needs to establish clear priorities to let people know what is important, through a business strategy or an operations strategy. Once priorities are set, if a new project gets added to the list, something else needs to be put on hold, or, as I often call it, put into the parking lot. Empower people to say "no" or at least ask, "If you want me to do this new thing, which of my current priorities would you like to delay?" Limiting high-priority tasks to three will help get things done.

To establish accountability, employees and their managers need to know who (and it should be *one* person) is responsible for a given task. If it is not accomplished, what *one* person will you talk to? I had a chance to ask a retired Air Force general what single action he took in his career to help people get things done, and he said that he always established accountability and measured results. When you assign tasks, establish how you will know that the task is complete, what measures you will use, and when the job will be completed by simply asking yourself, "Who is going to do what by when?"

The third way to make sure things get done is to follow up. George Patton, the commander of the third army for the United States during World War II, once said that many officers' biggest failing was not following up on the orders they gave. If you assign priorities and prepare measures but fail to follow up, people will soon figure out that you weren't serious and the work will not get done, especially if there is another project that is a competing priority or that they would rather work on.

The Components of Action

You might ask how an Action Imperative is different from Lean or other popular process and productivity improvement programs. First, an Action Imperative goes beyond problem solving toward progress and innovation. Many process improvement gurus suggest that problem solving is the foundation of change, but problem solving assumes a harmful deviation from the norm, requiring that the deviation be corrected to bring you back to the baseline. While that might be important for Lean, it doesn't move your company forward on the path to innovation and competitiveness.

Creating an Action Imperative is based on a combination of change management, continuous improvement, and culture reinforcement. It fosters innovation in processes and management to take your company to the next level. Combining change management with continuous improvement creates a stair-step pattern of innovation that leads to a new level of competitiveness.

Key Learning

Create operations discipline:

1. Make sure the systems and processes are well defined and constructed and have one owner.
2. Establish constructs and rules to keep things organized.
3. Develop behaviors through values and accountability.

To get things done:

1. Establish a few key priorities (preferably no more than three), and put the rest in the "parking lot."
2. Establish accountability with measures, including who (only one person) is accountable for the result.
3. Follow up.

Focus on change management, continuous improvement, and a culture of action.

To create an Action Imperative you need:

- A clear vision, a picture of the future that clarifies direction and motivates people.
- An overall champion for the process and the right people on the bus.
- A focus on continuous improvement, moving to the next level of performance.

CHAPTER 10

Implementing Operations Strategy

Most strategy fails at execution. Companies spend untold hours and several days off-site developing business and operations strategy, only to have the results languish on a shelf until the next planning cycle, usually a year away. Why don't they implement the great ideas and initiatives they spent so much time developing? In some cases it is a lack of initiative and follow-through, and in others a lack of accountability and discipline. In still others, they may not have the necessary talent or resources. Finally, it may come down to fear of change.

Conquering the Fear of Change

People seem to have an innate fear of the unknown. Does this policy change mean I or someone else screwed up? Is someone going to lose his or her job due to this process change? Will I look like a fool? Will I let my teammates down? Strategy implementation, at its core, is change. Helping people overcome their fear is part of management's role.

When I was young, change seemed to occur very slowly. I couldn't wait to move from grade school to junior high, then to get my driver's license, then to graduate from high school and college. Later in life, change seemed to happen so rapidly that it was like running downhill. I found that trying to cling to the past was not only disappointing, but just plain folly.

One client, Alaska Communications, asked me to help them develop a new supply chain strategy to reduce costs, reduce inventory, and improve customer service. During the project I often asked people why they were doing things a particular way, and the inevitable response was, "That's how we've always done it." Many employees had been at the company for over 30 years and change was scary to them. They believed that, if change was possible, it meant that their way of doing things was flawed, and no one likes to think they've been doing something wrong for 30 years.

When I was in high school, I lived in an area of the Rocky Mountains known for its rock climbing and mountaineering. I always felt that, if you were going to be an outdoors person, you needed to know how to swim and the basics of rock climbing. The only problem was that, when you got to the top of a particular rock face, the only practical way down was to rappel back down the face. Backing out over a 100-foot cliff with only a small rope keeping you from splattering on the rock below is terrifying. I panicked during the first two feet of the descent, but once I was partway down the face it was fun. When I got to the bottom, I would climb back up and do it again! Sometimes once you survive the first steps, change suddenly feels like something you can benefit from and even enjoy.

There are three things that help overcome the fear of change:

1. Have trusted partners.
2. Communicate a clear context.
3. Set a framework for change.

There is safety in numbers. Your partners in change can be your teammates, people in other departments, your suppliers, and even your customers. When Alaska Communications shared their vision for change with their suppliers, most of them enthusiastically signed on to help because the potential benefits were so great. As the partners got excited, so did the employees, and the fear began to evaporate.

The sponsors of change need to establish a clear vision and foundational values on which to build the environment of change. Helping employees understand why the changes are happening helps shift the focus from the past to the future and counteracts the assumption that change is needed only because someone screwed up. World-class athletes are always trying to improve regardless of the past performance. Tying the change to consistent company values helps everyone see how the change brings the company into better alignment with its mission, employees, and other stakeholders. The changes also need to be consistent with the business strategy and model to help set priorities during implementation.

Employees also need to know what the plan is and what is expected of them, which includes understanding priorities and next steps. At

Alaska Communications, we used my 12-point strategy (see Figure 4.1) as a guide, which clarified the process and reassured the employees. We brought suppliers and employees from other departments into the process early on so they knew what we were thinking and could add their input, which yielded an incredibly strong plan that everyone enthusiastically implemented with dramatic results.

It is important to make sure the following take place:

1. Measure results from the beginning. Many times the early results of the change can be the greatest, and you want to capture that to show the benefits of making the change.
2. Make sure there are early wins. While there is some debate as to whether to use pilot projects to roll out change, I believe that demonstrating that the new process works is important to building confidence. When I led change initiatives, I tried to select an area for initial implementation that (a) had a high likelihood of success, (b) was physically where others could see what was going on, and (c) was talked about in both formal and informal channels.
3. Celebrate victories so the change becomes fun. Celebrations can be food (often cited as the number one incentive), T-shirts, or hats identifying the team, and recognition at employee meetings.

These steps generate a feeling of "I want to be part of that," which then leads to wider rollout of the change.

Finally, be sure to put your best people in the teams for the initial change. In his book *American Commander*,[1] Ryan Zinke states that talent, motivation, and support are all necessary for any successful endeavor. He suggests that teams are comprised of the right people who learn by doing, and, with that experience, they can then train and lead others.

Role of Key Managers

For change to occur, first you need a strong directive, which comes from top management, usually an executive sponsor for the change. That

---

[1] Zinke, R., and S. McEwen. 2016. *American Commander, Serving a Country Worth Fighting For and Training the Brave Soldiers Who Lead The Way*. W Publishing Group.

directive or vision establishes why you are doing the change and where it will take you in terms of planned results. The directive needs to be clearly communicated and easily understood. It serves as the foundation for the project/team charter (see Appendix 2), enabling the change initiative.

Once the change flows into the middle management level, the day-to-day pressures of the business take hold, and change falters and can stop entirely. To prevent that, that top management needs to enable the middle management change champion to lead the change. I have found that, for every significant change effort I have been involved in, having a strong mid-level champion is critical for success. They are the ones that make it happen at the operations level by working directly with the ground-level change team and providing resources and leadership for the change. Top management needs to empower them by removing some of the day-to-day priorities to make time for the change initiative.

Looking Below the Waterline

Most companies think in terms of people, finance, markets, and technology when developing strategy and launching change initiatives. But, as shown in Figure 10.1, there are additional variables lurking below the surface.

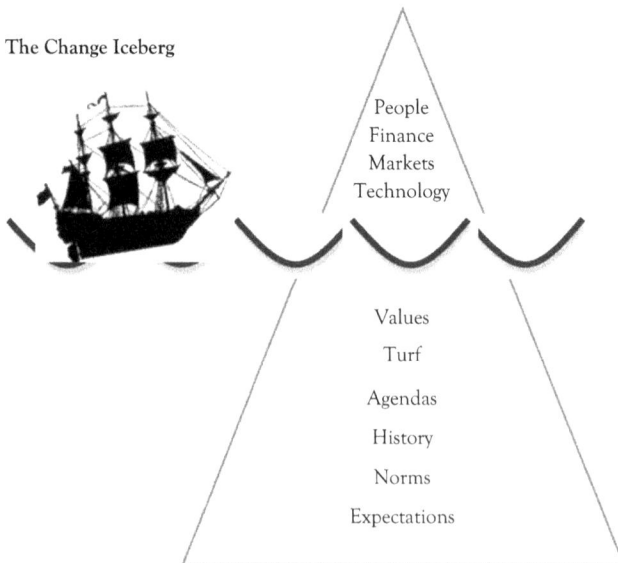

The Change Iceberg

People
Finance
Markets
Technology

Values
Turf
Agendas
History
Norms
Expectations

Figure 10.1 Variables lurk beneath the surface

The items below the water line are often the key pieces for success. Recognizing the values, turf, personal agendas, organization history, norms, and expectations can help smooth the road to change. Taking the time to recognize and deal with them can make all the difference.

In one client, the majority of the shop floor workers were Hispanic. I noticed that, when the manager and I were speaking to the team members involved in a Lean implementation in a particular area of the shop, the workers kept looking at an older gentleman who was usually standing in the back of the group. He wasn't a supervisor, but had been with the company for a long time. In Hispanic cultures, older people are revered and respected for their wisdom. The team was looking at him to see if he agreed with what we were saying. Once we discovered that, we included him in our planning to make sure he bought into the change. His support and influence were vital to our success.

People Make the Difference

In order to effectively move to the future state, you have to connect the organization and the people within it to the future. Figure 10.2 shows the factors involved.

Just considering the current state and the future state is not enough; the organization and its key components must be included in the process,

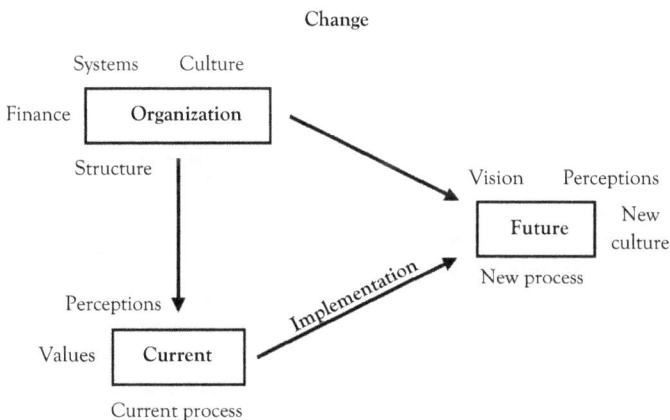

Figure 10.2 Connecting the organization and its people to the future

including the culture, structure, values, and perceptions of people at the lower levels of the organization.

At one client, we planned to overhaul the warehouse and distribution operations. A union ran the warehouses, and some of the work rules seemed to be roadblocks for the changes we wanted to make. For instance, one of the work rules was that no one but warehouse union members could touch inventory while it was in the warehouse, and we wanted to introduce vendor-managed inventory (VMI), which can be tough if the vendors can't even touch the bins to see what is in them. A full VMI system also includes the vendors restocking the shelves. The work rules set up a giant roadblock.

The union shop steward was also the warehouse supervisor. We invited her into our planning process and used the approach of "Do easy"[2] to show her how our proposed changes would make work easier for her and her crew. By showing her the benefits, we reached a compromise that allowed the suppliers to look in the bins for replenishment purposes, but not to restock. Her team kept that responsibility, at least initially. We also guaranteed that no one would be laid off due to the implementation of this change. A few were reassigned, but no one lost their job. Then, with the application of 5S, not only did the work get easier, but we created space to build a break area and clean up the warehouse, making the work environment significantly better. She was happy, her crew was happy, the union was happy, and we saved millions of dollars in productivity.

In *Good to Great: Why Some Companies Make the Leap and Others Don't*, author Jim Collins talks about having the right people on the bus. When you are implementing the operations strategy, this applies to people at all levels in the organization. Top management sets the vision, middle management is the change champion, and the people on the front lines are the ones that actually make the day-to-day changes that move the organization to new levels of performance. It is appropriate to make sure the right people are on the bus in order to achieve the results in your vision, starting with the hiring process, which should include not only the

---

[2] "Doing your tasks in the easiest, most relaxed way possible, which is also the quickest and most efficient way." From the short film *Discipline of Do Easy*, by Gus Van Sant, based on a short story by William S. Burroughs.

Results pyramid

Figure 10.3 The foundational levels that lead to excellent results

skills you need, but also traits, values, and personality that fit the culture. In addition, the review process needs to reinforce those traits and values to hold everyone accountable for the results.

Having good processes executed by good people with clear expectations and feedback will produce the results you plan for in your strategy. That results in a win/win for all of the stakeholders. Figure 10.3 illustrates the foundational levels that lead to excellent results.

Accelerating Profit and Growth

The three elements for accelerating profit and growth are like a three-legged stool, which offers the advantage of stability on any surface, off-set by the risk that, if a single leg fails, the stool collapses. To accelerate profit and growth, businesses rely on three "legs": framework, ideas, and people. When all three legs are present and functioning well, companies can accelerate into the express lanes. Figure 10.4 shows the possible outcomes if one of the three legs is faulty or missing.

The framework is the road map to the future state set by company leaders. Many leadership experts suggest that employees are more likely to get on board with change when they know where they are going and why. A clear framework fosters effective followership and better execution. Companies who lack a sound framework are wandering in the wilderness, hoping for results but never attaining them.

Accelerating profit and growth

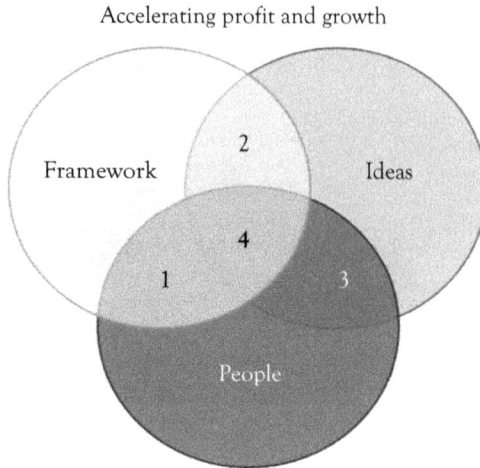

1. Stalled engine
2. No traction
3. Wandering in the wilderness
4. Accelerating profit and growth

Figure 10.4 The three elements needed for profit and growth

The ideas are the innovative, sometimes disruptive thinking that takes the company beyond the normal competitive advantage, sweeping them into the express lanes to speed past their competitors. These ideas come from throughout the organization, but usually materialize at the management levels, where innovators in the organization sponsor new, inventive ideas ranging from Lean to partnerships and more. They are the people who drive change, keep it on track, and bridge the gap between the executive visionaries and the front lines. Without ideas, a company is like a stalled engine and nothing gets accomplished.

People are the third leg of the stool. The process must be personalized to the people at all levels in the organization, all of whom have vital roles in implementing the strategy. Whether talent comes from inside or outside the organization is an important consideration that is often overlooked. Outsiders can bring in new thinking and fresh ideas, which is often why companies hire consultants. You can educate and develop your own people, but the time it takes may cost the competitive advantages of acceleration.

Internal skills can provide the advantage of sustainability, which is one reason why, in my consulting work, I always try to implement through the client's people rather than bringing in lower-level staff of my own. This approach allows the company's people to learn and gain experience, helping to sustain the change over time. It becomes their process, not mine.

A balance of internal and external resources can provide significant lift to the rapid instantiation of ideas and change. One client achieved dramatic results in just six months by using external resources, using internal leadership, and bringing the first-line people onboard early in the change process. If you have the framework and the ideas but weak or wrong people, you have no traction.

Leonardo da Vinci said that "simplicity is the ultimate sophistication." Simplifying the complex creates speed, a critical component of value. Eliminating complexity in whatever form it takes—overapplication of technology, excess process steps, communication across time zones, long cycle times, or even the number of suppliers you have—improves your ability to keep your promises to your customers quickly, with higher quality and lower cost. By designing your products, processes, or services for speed, you can create competitive advantage that helps move your company into the express lanes.

Some of the best measures are not numbers. Reputation, trust, and relationship speak loudly for your work with your partners both inside and outside the company. My friend Val Wright, author of *Thoughtfully Ruthless: The Key to Exponential Growth*, suggests the following self-assessment exercise:

1. List the three traits that set your company apart from your competitors.
2. Find out what sound bites or phrases your company is known for. I believe that speed, reliability, quality, and partnerships should lead the list.

Innovation forms a cornerstone of business vision and operations strategy. Innovation can come in two forms:

- Transformative innovation
- Transubstantial innovation

Transformative innovation takes what you have now and makes it better; it is creative improvement in product design, extensions, and Lean initiatives. Transubstantial innovation, on the other hand, creates something totally new, fundamentally changing the substance of the company. Ford was a transubstantial company, and so was Apple. Is your company?

By aligning the business vision with the operations strategy, you develop strength in both the vision, the where are we going and why model of the business as well as the how of the business. The vision is the engine that pulls and the operations strategy is the engine that pushes you in the express lanes of business toward dramatic profit and growth.

Key Learning

- Most strategy fails at execution. Why?
    - Lack of follow-through
    - Lack of discipline
    - Lack of talent and resources
    - Fear of change
- How to overcome fear:
    - Have trusted partners.
    - Communicate clear context.
    - Set the framework for change.
- Make sure the following take place:
    - Measure results from the beginning.
    - Make sure there are early wins.
    - Celebrate success.
- Middle-level managers are key to success.
- People make the difference—culture, perceptions, values, and structure.
- Framework, disruptive ideas, and personalization accelerate profit and growth.

APPENDIX 1

ABC Company
Develop Supply Chain Network Model
Task Force Charter

Task Force Purpose

To develop and recommend the centralized/branch purchasing and inventory management model for the company

Team Structure

Membership is comprised of:

- John Smith—chair
- Rick Pay—consultant
- Chris Columbus—controller
- Mike Jones—credit manager
- Dave Anderson—accounts payable

Team Objectives

- Prepare and confirm vision for purchasing and inventory management.
- Move company toward global (company-wide) coordination with local control.
- Identify roles and responsibilities for purchasing and inventory management including logistics and warehousing, and obsolete inventory.
- Establish accountability and ownership.
- Make recommendations for short-term material cost savings (e.g., new supplier model).
- Prepare communication plan and conduct training.

- ID key measures to drive accountability and establish one- to three-year targets.
- Create an organization that shifts price/buying leverage toward the company from suppliers by presenting a unified front with a cooperative approach.
- Recommend policy and internal controls as appropriate.
- Consider whether regional models make sense.

Time Frame

Initial design complete by March 15, 2011.
Implementation complete by May 1, 2011.

APPENDIX 2

Operations Strategy Sample Format

Following is a sample format for an operations strategy framework. It is from a real middle market manufacturer with the names and some details changed to mask the company. Note how brief it is and how it establishes priorities for action. It assumes there will be a series of task forces created for implementation, all reporting to a leadership task force who will monitor activity and establish accountability. Also note how the culture and values of the company are called out in the initial parts of the framework.

The plan starts with the company priorities, which would come from the vision and strategy covering the same period of time. The operations opportunities then create the structure for establishing priorities. The strategy elements are from the operations puzzle and cover those issues that are significant to the company for the period covered by the plan. Note there are only four high-priority items, and the rest are effectively in the parking lot for future action.

ABC Company Operations Framework for 2014/2015

Foundations for Strong Operations Strategy

1. Leverage each other
2. All working together
3. Use partners in growth
   a. They assist us
   b. They work for us
4. Engage at the global level
   a. How do we bridge local and global?
   b. What is the best use of the Asia sourcing offices?

Scope

Balance of 2014 and 2015

Company Priorities

Following are priorities for the company and for operations management

- Mission:
  - o High-value partnerships
  - o Taking advantage of new opportunities
  - o Innovative products
  - o Leveraging engineering/design
- Values:
  - o Service—customers, employees, company putting others first
  - o Make business easy!—Lean, simplification
  - o Create opportunities for employees
  - o Profitable and long-term focused—create cash flow
  - o Teamwork and fun
- Our business
  - o Quality—99.75 percent acceptance rate (now 99.1 percent)
  - o Price—competitive but not necessarily lowest
  - o Service
    - Put at highest level
    - Most responsive in industry
    - Immediate acknowledgment—lead time
    - 24-hour price confirmation
    - Stocking agreements—more customers asking for them
  - o Customer
    - Mid-sized OEM ($250 to $750 million annual sales)
    - Geography
      - West coast
      - Seattle is expanding
      - Adding Rocky Mountain West
      - No offshore support in foreseeable future

- o 2014 to 2015 goals
  - ▪ Grow Mexican production
  - ▪ Improve quality, cost, and delivery
  - ▪ Achieve profit and cash flow plans
- o Supporting goals
  - ▪ Quality certification
  - ▪ Increased responsiveness
    - • Quoting
    - • New product introduction
    - • Capable to promise
    - • On-time delivery—goal 95 percent (now 90 percent)
    - • Quality
  - ▪ Lean—reinvigorate
  - ▪ Business development—growing southwest
  - ▪ Process—improved communication with reps
- • Operations opportunities
  - o Timely, accurate information
    - ▪ Immediate pricing and lead times
    - ▪ Supply chain issues into hands of customers (e.g., allocations)
  - o Cost reduction
    - ▪ Includes overhead
    - ▪ Purchase price variance (PPV) is currently the big measure
    - ▪ Packaging
  - o Bonding programs
  - o Timely/competitive quoting—especially for make-to-order
  - o Business development assistance
    - ▪ Better relationships with suppliers
    - ▪ How to measure
    - ▪ How they help us grow
  - o Capable to promise
  - o Inventory and warehouse management
    - ▪ Discipline and focus
    - ▪ Stop being a victim
    - ▪ Improve strength of first in first out (FIFO) management

- Constraints
  - Customer-designated suppliers
    - Limits consolidation opportunities
    - Customer items are very expensive
  - Compliance—regulation issues are growing
  - Lot control—do we need it?
- Priorities:
  - Responsiveness
  - Make it easy
- Final thoughts
  - Think big; company-wide; entire value chain
  - What could be?
  - Leverage—team, suppliers, IT
  - Make it easy!

Priority of Key Issues

1. Quality
2. Delivery
3. Price/cost
4. Growth
5. Flexibility

Operations Strengths & Weaknesses

- Strengths:
  - People—dedicated and knowledgeable
  - Supplier relationships
  - Supporting production (parts on time)
  - Bonding programs (suppliers hold stock)
  - Flexibility (able to expedite)
  - Robust purchasing—Asia sourcing; better costs
  - New enterprise resource planning (ERP)
  - Growth potential—global
  - Manufacturing engineering team

- Weaknesses:
    - Lack of information used for quotes (e.g., accurate bills of materials)
    - Part numbers not the same across plants
    - Islands/lack of supply chain cohesion
    - Ability to transfer information inside and outside the organization
    - Proving higher PPV is better
    - Non-utilized buying power across locations
    - Highly tactical
    - Lack of supplier management
    - Logistics—hidden costs
    - Conflicting expectations
    - Unattainable metrics—what is important?
    - How to leverage/measure Asia sourcing performance
    - Low-level buying ("here is the PO, send the parts")
    - Geography (Asia) makes it difficult to control suppliers

Operations Management Objectives

- Responsiveness
- Predictable
- Reliable
- Profitable
- Useable
- Leverage
- Make it easy

Strategy Elements

Purpose of strategy is focus and direction

- How to deliver value
- Develop trust/decisions at the right level
- Teamwork
- Focus on people first, then ideas, then technology in that order

Higher-priority Elements

1. Supply chain/materials
   a. Supplier rationalization
   b. Lead time predictability
   c. Offshore total cost of ownership management
   d. Customer owned inventory management and control
   e. Freight costs
   f. FIFO management
2. Business processes
   a. BOM management
   b. Part number management
   c. Ramp down processes
   d. Quoting
   e. Part change notice/Engineering change notice component life-cycle notice from suppliers
   f. Asia sourcing
   g. Information sharing
   h. Part master management
   i. Regulation
   j. Business divisions
   k. Supplier certification and audit
   l. Auto-replenishment systems
3. Organization and management (reporting structure, roles, rewards)
   a. How organized (by commodity, customer)?
   b. How coordinated across locations (consistency)?
   c. Development of supplier business manager role
   d. Right-sized
   e. How to obtain capacity?
   f. How to back up for vacations and other needs
4. Production technology
   a. Electronic data interchange (EDI)/Materials requirements planning (MRP) data share
   b. Accounts Payable invoice processes

Lower-priority Elements

1. IT
    a. MRP suggestions—make meaningful, consistent, and understandable
2. Vertical integration
    a. None
3. Capacity
    a. Need predictability
    b. Supplier onboarding process
4. Facilities
    a. Cage security (Canby)
    b. Facility security (Tecate—metals security)
    c. ITAR (International traffic in arms regulations) compliance
5. Workforce (wages and skills)
    a. Need formal training programs
    b. Right-sized
6. Metrics/accountability
    a. Develop channels of communication with corporate/executives
    b. Measures
        i. Shipped-on-time
        ii. Turns
        iii. Accuracy
        iv. Cost out
        v. Purchase lead time/predictability
        vi. Supplier consolidation/count
7. Risk management
    a. Needs assessment

Implementation

Change Management

Executive sponsor—George Washington
Champion—James Madison

Task Force Development

A series of task forces will be used to implement the aforementioned. Each task force will have a leader/champion, a charter, and measures of success. Action plans will be developed with anticipated activities over a short period of time.

- Task forces may be made up of cross-location personnel
- TF will encourage participation at all levels
- TF will encourage cross-functional efforts with mutual objectives
- TF meetings will use effective meeting practices and may be conducted via Hangout, Skype, Zoom, or phone

Next Steps

1. Develop leadership team for ongoing guidance/monitoring of task forces
2. Identify top priorities and kick off task forces to address
   a. BOM accuracy for quotes/NPI, duplicate part numbers, other issues; has big impact on responsiveness
   b. Cross-location supply chain organization and coordination
   c. Supplier rationalization
   d. Cross-location part number management
3. Next-level priorities:
   a. To be determined
4. Develop operations dashboards to track progress
5. Flesh out operations management plan (central coordination with local control?) and levels of cooperation between locations
   a. Develop inventory management strategy
   b. Review product architecture for impacts
      i. Variability and volume of demand
      ii. Predictability of supply
      iii. Clock speed of products (how fast do they change)
      iv. Lead time

Remember—Success, Not Perfection!

About the Author

Rick Pay has been dubbed by his clients as the "Sherlock Holmes of Operations and Supply Chain Management." He is the Principal and Founder of The R. PAY COMPANY, LLC, a consulting firm established in 1999 to help mid-market companies accelerate profit and growth through leading-edge business and operations strategy, profitable partnerships, and operations and supply chain excellence. His clients are rapidly growing manufacturing, distribution, retail, telecommunications, high tech, and professional service firms.

Rick's book, *1 + 1 = 100: Achieving Breakthrough Results Through Partnerships*, was published in December 2016 by Business Expert Press. Rick appears frequently as a speaker, and his articles have been published by Industry Week, the Institute for Supply Management, Supply Chain World, and others. He has been interviewed and quoted in publications including Forbes, National Foundation of Independent Business (NFIB), and CFO Magazine.

Rick holds a BS from Colorado State University and an MBA focusing on Business Systems from the University of Montana. He has attended executive programs at Stanford University and MIT, mentors other consultants, and belongs to Alan Weiss's Million Dollar Consulting Hall of Fame.

Index

OTHER TITLES IN OUR SUPPLY AND OPERATIONS MANAGEMENT COLLECTION

Joy M. Field, Boston College, Editor

- *Contemporary Issues in Supply Chain Management and Logistics* by Anthony M.Pagano and Mellissa Gyimah
- *Understanding the Complexity of Emergency Supply Chains* by Matt Shatzkin
- *Mastering Leadership Alignment: Linking Value Creation to Cash Flow* by Jahn Ballard and Andrew Bargerstock
- *Statistical Process Control for Managers, Second Edition* by Victor Sower
- *Sustainable Operations and Closed Loop Supply Chains, Second Edition* by Gilvan Souza
- *The High Cost of Low Prices: A Roadmap to Sustainable Prosperity* by David S. Jacoby

Announcing the Business Expert Press Digital Library

Concise e-books business students need for classroom and research

This book can also be purchased in an e-book collection by your library as

- a one-time purchase,
- that is owned forever,
- allows for simultaneous readers,
- has no restrictions on printing, and
- can be downloaded as PDFs from within the library community.

Our digital library collections are a great solution to beat the rising cost of textbooks. E-books can be loaded into their course management systems or onto students' e-book readers.

The **Business Expert Press** digital libraries are very affordable, with no obligation to buy in future years. For more information, please visit **www.businessexpertpress.com/librarians**. To set up a trial in the United States, please email **sales@businessexpertpress.com**.